FEEDING A YEN

RANDOM HOUSE · NEW YORK

FEEDING A YEN

To Sheila,

Calvin Trillin

SAVORING LOCAL
SPECIALTIES,
FROM KANSAS CITY
TO CUZCO

CALVIN TRILLIN

LIBRARY OF CONGRESS CATALOGING-IN-PUBLICATION DATA

Trillin, Calvin.

Feeding a yen : savoring local specialties, from Kansas City to Cuzco / Calvin Trillin.

p.   cm.

ISBN 0-375-50808-2

1. Cookery, American.   2. Trillin, Calvin.   I. Title.

TX715.T775 2003

641.5973—dc21   2002037055

Parts of this book appeared originally, in different form, in *The New Yorker, Gourmet,* and other magazines.

Printed in the United States of America on acid-free paper

Random House website address: atrandom.com

2 4 6 8 9 7 5 3

FIRST EDITION

Book design by Barbara M. Bachman

For more than thirty-five years, my companion

at the table was my wife, Alice.

Although I did once describe Alice as having

"a weird predilection for limiting our family

to three meals a day," her knowledge and enjoyment

of food had a lot to do with the pleasure I took

in writing about eating. Partway through this book's

adventures, which took place over several years,

her name no longer appears.

She died in September 2001. I know she would have

expected this dedication to be shared with our

first grandchild, Isabelle Alice Trillin-Lee, who,

as it happens, has already

shown signs of being a good eater.

CONTENTS

FEEDING A YEN

1.

MAGIC BAGEL

≡

Not long after the turn of the millennium, I had an extended father-daughter conversation with my older daughter, Abigail, on the way back from a dim sum lunch in Chinatown. Abigail, who was living in San Francisco, had come to New York to present a paper at a conference. As a group of us trooped back toward our house in Greenwich Village, where she'd grown up, Abigail and I happened to be walking together. "Let's get this straight, Abigail," I said, after we'd finished off some topic and had gone along in silence for a few yards. "If I can find those gnarly little dark pumpernickel bagels that we used to get at Tanenbaum's, you'll move back to New York. Right?"

"Absolutely," Abigail said.

There's a great comfort in realizing that a child you've helped rear has grown up with her priorities straight. When I phoned Abigail from the Oakland airport once to ask if she knew of an alternative route to her house in San Francisco— I'd learned of a huge traffic jam on the normal route, toward the Bay Bridge—she said, "Sure. Go south on 880, take 92 west across the bridge to 101, and we'll meet you at Fook Yuen for lunch." Fook Yuen is a dim sum restaurant in Millbrae, about five minutes from the San Francisco airport, and its way with a dumpling has persuaded us that flights in and out of San Francisco are best scheduled in the middle of the day. I report this response to a traffic jam as a way of demonstrating not simply that Abigail always has a fallback career as a taxi dispatcher awaiting her but also that she has the sort of culinary standards that could induce her to switch coasts if the right bagel came along.

But when I mentioned the Chinatown walk exchange to my wife, Alice, she had a different interpretation. She said that Abigail had been speaking ironically. I found it difficult to believe that anybody could be ironic about those bagels. They were almost black. Misshapen. Oniony. Abigail had always adored them. Both of my daughters have always taken bagels seriously. When my younger daughter, Sarah, was a little girl, I revealed in print that she wouldn't go to Chinatown without carrying a bagel—"just in case." At the time that Abigail and I had our conversation about the gnarly black pumpernickel bagel, Sarah was also living in California, in Los Angeles. She seemed perfectly comfortable with the Chinese food there. In fact, when I'd eaten with her at Chinois on Main, in Santa Monica, it occurred to me that her knowledge of the menu was nearly encyclopedic. She had many years before outgrown the need to have a bagel with her at a Chinese restaurant—which was fortunate indeed, because bagels in California were not anywhere near up to her standards.

For a while, I brought along a dozen or two New York bagels for Sarah whenever I went to Southern California, but I finally decided that this policy was counterproductive. "If a person prefers to live in California, which happens to be thousands of miles from her very own family," I told her, "it seems to me appropriate that such a person eat California bagels. I understand that in some places out there if you buy a dozen wheat germ bagels you get your choice of a bee pollen bagel or a ginseng bagel free." Sarah eventually moved back East. I'm not going to make any claims for the role of my bagel-withholding policy in that decision, but the fact remains: she did eventually move back East.

I have previously recorded Abigail's response, at age four or five, when, on a visit to my family in Kansas City, Missouri, she'd worked her way partly through a bagel I can describe, given my affection for my hometown, as an honest effort that had simply fallen way short of the mark, the baker having been put in the position a New York deli cook would have found himself in if asked to turn out a bowl of andouille gumbo. "Daddy," she said, "how come in Kansas City the bagels taste like just round bread?" In other words, she knew the difference between those bagel-shaped objects in the Midwest and the authentic New York item that had been hand-rolled and boiled in a vat and then carefully baked by a member in good standing of the Bakery and Confectionery Workers International Union. I think it might be fair to characterize her as having been a bagel prodigy.

When I was a child, bagel consumption in Kansas City was not widespread. Bagels were thought of as strictly Jewish food, eaten mainly in New York. In those days, of course, salsa would have been considered strictly Mexican food, if anybody I knew in Kansas City had ever given any consideration to salsa. I doubt if many gentiles in Kansas City had ever heard of a bagel, let alone eaten one. Bagels were available in only two or three stores, one of which was called the New York Bakery. It was only in the real New York that bagels were part of the culture, for both Jews and gentiles. New Yorkers have always talked about picking up freshly baked bagels late at night and being reassured, as they felt the warmth coming through the brown paper bag, that they would be at peace with the world the next morning, at least through breakfast. They've talked about that day in the park when nothing seemed to soothe their crying baby until a grandmotherly woman sitting on a nearby bench, nattering with another senior citizen about Social Security payments or angel food cake recipes or Trotskyism, said that the only thing for a teething infant was a day-old bagel. They've talked about the joy of returning to New York from a long sojourn in a place that was completely without bagels— Indonesia or a tiny town in Montana or some other outpost in the vast patches of the world that New Yorkers tend to think of as the Bagel Barrens.

Roughly corresponding to the time it took our girls to grow up and move to California, bagels had become assimilated. Gefilte fish was still Jewish food, but not bagels. The bagel had gone from a regional ethnic food to an American standard, served at McDonald's and available on supermarket shelves all over the part of America that baked-goods sociologists have long identified with white bread. At one point, I read that, because of a new plant established by one of the firms producing supermarket bagels, the state that led all other American states in turning out bagels was Iowa. A couple of years before Abigail and I discussed pumpernickel bagels on the way back from Chinatown, *The New York Times* had run a piece by Suzanne Hamlin reporting that in places recently introduced to bagels, emergency rooms were seeing an increasing number of bagel-related injuries—cuts, gouges, and severed digits caused by "impatient eaters who try to pry apart frozen bagels with screwdrivers, attempt to cut hard bagels with dull knives and, more than likely, use their palms as cutting boards." There had been no increase in New York bagel injuries.

From the *Times* story, you could draw the conclusion that a lot of Americans were being given access to bagels before they knew how to handle them, in the way that a lot of Americans are said to have access to 9-mm pistols or semiautomatic rifles before they know how to handle them. I suspect any number of New Yorkers responded to the story by saying, in the superior tone customarily used by someone from Minneapolis who's relating the chaos caused in Birmingham by a simple snowstorm, "People there just don't have any experience in such things"—or, as the director of emergency medicine at Bellevue did say to the *Times,* "Those people just aren't ethnically equipped."

Aside from the safety issue, the mainstreaming of formerly ethnic or regional food like bagels must have been confusing for those citizens who grew up before it became common to find Cajun restaurants in upper midwestern shopping malls and lobster shacks in Amarillo. In the eighties, when it was revealed that eating poppy-seed bagels could result in a false positive on a drug test, I saw one of the perils inherent in everybody's suddenly eating everything, whether ethnically equipped or not. I envisioned an applicant to the FBI academy who seems in the tradition of the bureau: he's a well-set-up young man with a square jaw and a direct gaze. He's almost maddeningly polite. His name is O'Connor. He went to Fordham. He always wears a suit and a white shirt and wing-tipped shoes. His father was in the bureau. His drug test seems to indicate that he's a user.

O'Connor is looking stunned. "I can't understand it," he says. "Maybe it was something I ate."

"Oh, yeah, I'm sure that was it," the tester, a grizzled agent near retirement age, says sarcastically. "We all know how corned beef and cabbage can mess up these results."

"You don't think it could have been those chiles rellenos I had for lunch, do you?" O'Connor says, ignoring the sarcasm. "That pico de gallo that came with them was pretty hot stuff."

"Maybe you can catch on with the Parks Department, O'Connor," the tester says, in a more sympathetic tone. "Or Sanitation. You're a husky lad."

"I can't believe blackened redfish would do it," O'Connor says. "Maybe it was that braised bok choy I had with my squid last night. That's all I've eaten lately, except for the poppy-seed bagels with lox and cream cheese that Father Sweeney served at the Holy Name Society breakfast this morning."

"The dope is making you talk crazy, son," the tester says.

The sad part is that they would have almost certainly been inferior poppy-seed bagels. Provisions for the Holy Name

Society breakfast might well have been purchased at the local supermarket or at one of those places that make bagels with weird ingredients—blueberries, say, and cinnamon, and more air than you'd find in a Speaker of the House. O'Connor, not having been raised in the connoisseurship, probably wouldn't have known the difference. Not so my daughters. When they were children, bagels were not only their staple food—the food they clung to in unfamiliar surroundings—but also the food used in important rituals. On Sunday mornings, I often took them to Houston Street, on the Lower East Side. At Russ & Daughters, which is what New Yorkers refer to as an appetizing store, we would buy Nova Scotia salmon. Then we'd go next door to Ben's Dairy to get cream cheese and a delicacy known as baked farmer's cheese with scallions. Then we were at Tanenbaum's, a bakery that was probably best known for a large, dark loaf often referred to as Russian health bread. We were not there for Russian health bread. We were there for Abigail's pumpernickel bagels. Abigail had never exhibited any irony when the subject was pumpernickel bagels. Would Proust have been ironic about the madeleine, particularly if he had fetched up in a place where you couldn't get a decent madeleine if your life depended on it?

"So you think she's just humoring her old dad?" I asked Alice, during our discussion of the bagel conversation I'd had with Abigail on the way back from Chinatown.

"I do."

Alice was probably right. I understood that. Abigail was enjoying California, and she had a job there that she loved. As I've admitted before, my daughters have simply made good on their implicit threat to grow up and lead lives of their own.

Parents are supposed to accept that. Still, I decided that I'd look around for those pumpernickel bagels. As my father used to say, "What could it hurt?"

It wasn't my first try. When the pumpernickel bagels disappeared, I immediately made serious inquiries. Without wanting to cast blame, I have to say that the disappearance occurred on Mutke's watch. Mutke's formal name is Hyman Perlmutter. In the early seventies, he bought Tanenbaum's Bakery and transformed it into the downtown branch of a bakery he ran eight or ten blocks away called Moishe's. For some time, Mutke carried Tanenbaum's full inventory. Then, one day—I don't remember precisely when, but Abigail and Sarah were still living at home—the pumpernickel bagels were no longer there. Confronted with the facts, Mutke was sanguine. Those particular bagels weren't available anymore, he explained, but, as a special order, he could always provide me with a dozen or two just like them. Eventually, he did. I pulled one out of the bag. It was a smooth bagel, uniformly round. It was the color of cappuccino, heavy on the milk. It was a stranger to onions. It was not by any means Abigail's bagel.

I realize now, of course, that I gave up too easily. Sure, I stopped by to try the pumpernickel any time I heard of a promising new bagel bakery—even if it was uptown, a part of the city I don't venture to unnecessarily. But I didn't make a systematic, block-by-block search. I didn't make the pumpernickel bagel my number-one priority. How was I to know that bagels can be instrumental in keeping families intact? This time, I was going to be thorough. I'd read in Molly O'Neill's *New York Cook Book* about a place in Queens where bagels were made in the old-fashioned way. I figured that there must be similar places in Brooklyn neighborhoods with large populations of Orthodox Jews—Williamsburg, maybe, or Borough Park. I was prepared to go to the outer boroughs. But I thought it made sense to start back on Houston Street.

The area where Abigail and Sarah and I used to make our Sunday rounds has seen some changes over the years. The old tenement streets had once seemed grim, but at some point in the nineties they began to sport patches of raffish chic. On Orchard Street, around the corner from our Sunday-morning purveyors, stores that traditionally offered bargains on fabrics and women's clothing and leather goods became punctuated by the sort of clothing store that has a rack of design magazines and a coffee bar and such a spare display of garments hanging on exposed-brick walls that you might think you're in the studio apartment of someone who has rather bizarre taste in cocktail dresses and no closet to keep them in. At some point the Lower East Side became a late-night destination—both Orchard and Ludlow acquired bars too hip to need signs—and a cool place to live. Around the time I started looking for the pumpernickel bagel in earnest, an apartment on one of the old tenement blocks of Orchard Street changed hands for a million dollars. I could only hope for the new owner's sake that his old *zayde* wasn't still alive ("You paid what! To live in a place we worked sixteen hours a day to get out of you paid what!"). After spending years listening to customers tell him that he ought to move Russ & Daughters uptown, Mark Federman—the grandson of Joel Russ, the founder—was renovating the apartments above the store and expressing gratitude that his grandfather had held on to the building.

Ben's Dairy had closed and Moishe's Bakery had moved to a tiny place around the corner. But Russ & Daughters has been carefully preserved to look pretty much the way it did when Joel Russ himself still had his arms deep into the herring barrel. I figured Mark might have some information I could use, and he was bound to be sympathetic to the project: his daughter, Niki, had recently graduated from college and moved to San Francisco. "Do you think Niki might come back, too, if we found the bagels?" I asked, as Mark and I edged ourselves into the tiny office he shares with his wife, Maria.

"I don't think she'd come back for bagels," he said. "Maybe for an apartment upstairs."

Maria shook her head. "I already offered," she said.

Mark said he knew precisely the bagel I was talking about, but he had no idea where to find it. He phoned his mother, one of the daughters of Russ & Daughters, who had retired to Florida. "Do you remember when Tanenbaum next door used to have this sort of gnarly—" he began, and then started to laugh. "Not an old woman," he said. "I'm asking about bagels." Apparently, his mother remembered the gnarly old woman quite well. Not the bagels.

Although Russ & Daughters now carries bagels, Mark insisted that he didn't have the expertise to be much help in tracing a particular baker; locating an obscure source of belly lox would have been more his line of country. Still, he made a couple of calls, including one to Mosha's Bread, a wholesale operation in Williamsburg, which has been turning out pumpernickel since the late nineteenth century. (Mosha's Bread, it almost goes without saying, has no connection with Moishe's Bakery.) As I was about to leave Russ's, the boss of Mosha's, who turned out to be a woman named Cecile Erde Farkas, returned Mark's call. Mark introduced himself, and before he could explain my quest he began to sound like someone on the receiving end of a sales pitch. "To tell you the truth, I don't sell much bread," I heard him say, and then, "Here's what I could use—a good babka. I could sell the hell out of a good babka . . . plain, yeah, and chocolate."

There was a message on my answering machine that evening from Mark. He had reached a friend of his named Danny Scheinin, who'd run Kossar's, a distinguished purveyor of bialys, for decades before selling out a year or two before. "Danny says he thinks Tanenbaum got that bagel from somebody named Poznanski," Mark said, when I got back to him. "Also, he says it wasn't a real bagel."

"Not a real bagel!"

"I don't know exactly what he means," Mark said. "Talk to him."

When I reached Scheinin, I found out that what he'd meant was this: in the old days, there was a sharp split between bagel bakeries and bread bakeries. The bagel bakers had their own local, No. 338. They didn't bake bread and bread bakers didn't make bagels. Originally, of course, bagels were made only with white flour. But some bread bakers who trafficked in pumpernickel would twist some bread dough into bagel shapes and bake them. By not going through the intermediate boiling that is part of the process of making an authentic bagel, they stayed out of another local's jurisdiction. Scheinin was confident that Abigail's bagel had been made that way for Tanenbaum's by a bread baker named Sam Poznanski, in Williamsburg, who had been dead for some years. As far as Scheinin knew, the bakery still existed, under the management of Poznanski's wife. He gave me the number. "Tell her Danny from the bialys said to call," he told me.

Mrs. Poznanski, I have to say, did not seem terribly engaged by my quest, even after I explained to her what a splendid young woman Abigail had grown up to be—partly, presumably, thanks to a steady diet of bagels baked by the late Sam Poznanski—and how much I'd like to have her back in New York. The longest answer I got was when I asked Mrs. Poznanski if the bakery had quit making the pumpernickel bagel when her husband died, and she said, "No. Before." Still, she confirmed that the object of Abigail's adoration was from Poznanski's and that it was not boiled. This was hard news to take. It sounded perilously close to saying that the bagel we were searching for was just round bread. But what bread!

The bread-bagel split was confirmed by Herb Bostick, a business agent of Local 3 of the Bakery and Confectionery Workers Union, which had absorbed No. 338 into a local that mixes bagel bakers and bread bakers and cake bakers together the way someone faced with baking a pie at the last minute might mix in bits of whatever kinds of flour happened to be in the cupboard. What Bostick said was in line with what I'd learned from Cecile Farkas, of Mosha's, with whom I'd arranged a meeting after her babka pitch to Mark. She'd told me that for years her late father offered pumpernickel bagels that were baked without being boiled first. "Then they weren't real bagels?" I'd said.

"If my daddy called them bagels they were bagels," Mrs. Farkas said.

I hadn't had to venture to the outer boroughs to see Cecile Farkas. By chance, she was doing a bread promotion at a store on Twenty-third Street. She turned out to be a chatty woman in her sixties who told me that she had joined Mosha's only when her father became elderly; she'd been trained as an electrical engineer. That didn't surprise me. Mark Federman had practiced law for a while. A family business is no respecter of degrees. Mrs. Farkas told me that her own daughter, having earned her master's in career counseling, planned to launch Mosha's West. Would Mosha's West be a few blocks closer to Manhattan than the original Mosha's? No. The daughter lived in San Francisco. Having her own daughter at the other end of the country may have made Mrs. Farkas particularly empathetic to my situation. She said that, with a few hours' notice, Mosha's could turn out precisely the sort of bagel Abigail craved. "It would be my pleasure," she said.

"If that happens and Abigail moves back to New York, you would have done a mitzvah," I said. "It would be written next to your name in the Book of Life."

Mrs. Farkas shrugged off any thought of reward. "It

would be my pleasure," she repeated. I had recognized her as a person of character the moment she'd told me that whatever her daddy said was a bagel was a bagel.

I tried to present the situation to Alice in an objective way: "I suppose you think that if Mosha's really did succeed in duplicating the bagel and I told Abigail that it was readily available in the neighborhood and I didn't trouble her with the really quite arcane information that it's not, technically speaking, a bagel, I would be acting completely contrary to everything we tried to teach her about honesty and integrity."

"Yes," Alice said.

"I thought you might."

She was right, of course. I know that. Later, though, it occurred to me that there were areas I had left unexplored in my conversation with Mrs. Poznanski. It's true that she expressed no interest whatsoever in bagels, but what if I got Mark Federman to agree to carry those little pumpernickel numbers—not instead of Mrs. Farkas's babkas, I hasten to say, but in addition to Mrs. Farkas's babkas? Would the Russ & Daughters account be enough to propel Poznanski's back into the bagel business? This is assuming, of course, that Sam Poznanski's recipe still exists. While I was thinking about all of this, Niki Federman came back from San Francisco and moved into one of the newly renovated apartments over Russ & Daughters.

2

PEPPER CHASE

‗

I'm aware that I tend to go on about *pimientos de Padrón*. They are on a list I keep in my head of the victuals that, despite being my favorite dishes in one part of the world or another, rarely seem to be served outside their territory of origin— a list I sometimes refer to as the Register of Frustration and Deprivation. I have always assumed that a lot of people have such a list, no matter where they live. Now and then, I try to comfort myself with the thought that, given the fact that I live in New York, my Register of Frustration and Deprivation is much shorter than it would be if I lived anywhere else. That doesn't seem to help much.

When I think of food I've enjoyed in Tuscany, for instance, I think of the grain called farro—something that almost never seems to turn up on the menus of those Tuscan trattorias that gradually became more prevalent in Manhattan than delis. Of all the things I've eaten in the Cajun country of Louisiana—an array of foodstuffs which has been characterized as somewhere between extensive and deplorable—I yearn most often for boudin. Except when a kindly friend of mine from New Iberia arrives in New York carrying his ice chest, I've never had Cajun boudin outside of Louisiana. During long New York winters, no such kindly friend arrives from Nova Scotia, where I live in the summer, carrying an ice chest full of Lunenburg sausage, which is strong on the herb summer savory and can be grilled like a hot dog or eaten with Lunenburg County sauerkraut or crumbled in a pasta dish that has always been called at our house *spagatinni Lunenburgesa*. Lame versions of tapas are served all over New York, but none of the city's markets sell that bread rubbed with tomatoes that you get at La Boqueria, the splendid public market of Barcelona. My register is filled with dishes like that. On gray afternoons, I go over it, like a miser who is both tantalizing and tormenting himself by poring over a list of people who owe him money.

When, at the tag end of a long meal, people begin talking about their unsatisfied food cravings, my tale is often about *pimientos*. It always starts in Santiago de Compostela, which has been one of the world's great pilgrimage destinations for more than a millennium—the goal of pilgrims who demonstrate their devotion by walking for miles down El Camino de Santiago. The market, just a few blocks from the magnificent Romanesque cathedral that is said to hold the remains of St. James the Apostle, is about to open. It's early in the morning. The fishmongers are still lining up their sardines, and a butcher is using something that looks like a blowtorch to singe the last hairs from a hog's head. Scattered along one edge of the market, a dozen women from the town of Padrón itself, which is only fifteen miles away, sit behind huge baskets of digit-sized green peppers. They sort constantly, setting aside the peppers that they can distinguish, simply by touch, as unsuitably piquant, and preparing a couple of hundred-*pimiento* bags on the off chance that some customer in a terrible hurry will not want to witness the selection being counted out, pepper by pepper. I'm standing with something akin to a religious feeling in that lovely market, whose vaulted stone market sheds are actually called naves. I'm thinking about how the very peppers I'm observing are going to taste in a few hours, after they've been fried in olive oil and sprinkled with coarse salt, and my distress at having to wait those few hours is such that I have to nip over to the market-café across the street and buck myself up with some fresh *churros* dipped in *café con leche*.

"Peppers!" says someone at the table who has been itching to describe the exquisite pleasure of eating something drizzled with something on a bed of something else. "You're making all this fuss about some little green peppers cooked in oil? You *yearn* for peppers?"

I do. They're on the register.

By putting *pimientos de Padrón* on the list, I don't mean to imply that the region of Spain that Santiago serves as spiritual and political capital—Galicia, which the less sophisticated geographers usually describe as the bit above Portugal—is a one-dish spot. Galicians (*gallegos* in Spanish) gave the world, among other dishes, *caldo gallego,* the soup that is often the first item Cubans, many of whom are grandchildren of Galician migrants, put on their restaurants' menus. Galicians are renowned for their *empanadas*—absolutely flat pies that are filled with a layer of tuna or sardines or lamprey eel or pork. The Galician version of turnip greens provides a glorious piece of evidence that Galicia may have been visited in the past not only by the Vikings and Romans and Visigoths and Arabs and Normans and Celts mentioned in the guidebooks but also by some honest dirt farmers from Alabama.

Above all, Galicia has seafood of a variety and quality unmatched by any place I've ever been. In Galicia, a neighborhood café might offer among its snacks mussels, oysters, scallops, crawfish, three kinds of lobster, razor clams, spider crabs, ordinary crabs, octopus, squid, baby cuttlefish, clams, gooseneck barnacles (which, I have to say in the spirit of constructive criticism, might have been better off choosing another part of a goose to look like), and two or three varieties of shrimp. At practically any celebration, the presence of octopus is understood. I once read in a guidebook, for instance, that toward the end of June every year, at a shrine near a village called Silleda, people who feel themselves possessed by demons go through a ritual to exorcise the demons, and then everyone gathers for a feast of octopus. In Las Nieves, there is an annual celebration during which the families and friends of people who had a close brush with death the previous year march in a procession carrying tiny coffins and then join the assembled for a serious octopus feed. If bar mitzvahs are held in Galicia, I would expect to find octopus at the reception.

The seafood comes as a sort of surprise. In fact, the first time Alice and I were in that part of Spain—this was in the middle sixties, and we were driving through on our way to

Portugal—we somehow remained oblivious to the sorts of marine creatures that could be put on our plate. Maybe we were moving too fast to eat, although I remember stopping in Santiago at the Hostal Reyes Católicos, which was built in the sixteenth century as a shelter for pilgrims. What we had read and heard about Galicia was how green it was and how picturesque. In those days, it was, in fact, almost shamelessly picturesque. In Galicia, a haystack is conical—the point on top finished off with a flourish, like the top of a soft-ice-cream cone. Galician farmers have always managed to make works of art out of the necessities of farming—stone walls, for instance, and haystacks and, most of all, the simple granary. The granaries, or *hórreos,* are like small stone houses on stilts, with pitched tile roofs that are almost always adorned with stone crosses. At the time of that first visit, Franco had just appointed as tourist minister a man named Manuel Fraga Ibarne, who was said to be taking a more modern approach to marketing Spain's attractions, and a lot of what we saw looked perfect enough to have been staged by him personally. "Ah, clever of you to place that *hórreo* in silhouette against that stand of pine trees, Fraga Ibarne," we'd find ourselves commenting as we drove along a mountain road in Galicia. Passing an old woman who was dressed completely in black and was pulling along a cart of twigs, we might say, "Ah, back in your hardy-peasant drag, Fraga, you sly devil."

It was on our next trip, maybe twenty-five years later, that we got the full impact of the seafood. I felt like some traveler who, having put off visiting Italy for many years because he has a limited interest in old churches and restored hill towns, finally shows up and discovers, for the first time, that the Italians have a way with pasta. The temptation is to ask, Why didn't anybody tell me about this before?

By that second trip, of course, Fraga Ibarne's machinations were less in evidence. We had arrived in Vigo, a city of about 250,000 people, most of whom were honking their horns. It was lunchtime, and we had found an outdoor café in the port, on a short block called Calle Pescadores. Fraga Ibarne would have shuddered at the ambience. On one side of a narrow street were three or four cafés, with tables that permitted the customers to stare straight into the cement back wall of a hotel that looked ugly enough from the front. There were jagged holes in the wall where pipes came through. The only thing breaking the view of the cement wall was the stand of a clothes vendor who was selling what looked like Kmart castoffs. There were four vendors of a different sort on our side of the street, just in front of the cafés—women who stood behind marble tables and shucked oysters. They acted as independent operators, bringing oysters to customers at any of the cafés. It was the café operators' responsibility to furnish the lemons. Ours did bring lemons, along with a huge spider crab and some grilled shrimp and some bread and an order of *pimientos de Padrón*. I looked around at the view. Then I had another bite of crab, which was delicious. Then I had some more peppers. The peppers were truly wondrous. "You know," I finally said to Alice, "this place is beautiful in its own way."

Galicia, we discovered, is a grazer's paradise. In the narrow streets off Santiago's cathedral square, it is common to stop at a restaurant to have a *ración* (a healthy portion) of, say, razor clams and a *ración* of octopus and of sardines and, of course, of *pimientos de Padrón*—and then move on to the place next door or across the street, where the cuttlefish had seemed particularly succulent the previous evening, even though the *pimientos* were merely spectacular. It was in Galicia that I said to Alice, after what I suppose you might call a series of meals one evening, "Alice, I think we should break out of that old breakfast-lunch-dinner trap."

Galicians are great celebrators of food—actually, they're pretty good at celebrating just about anything—and it's not unusual for a town to have, say, a razor clam festival or a sardine festival or an *empanada* festival. Our second visit to Galicia was in late July, which should have been at the height of the festival season, but we'd apparently chosen the week when the celebrators paused to catch their breath. The blow that I found hardest to bear during that trip of lost opportunities was missing the *pimientos de Padrón* festival, held every year just outside Padrón in the tiny village of Herbón—the place whose monastery was where Franciscans apparently first tried growing the pepper seeds they'd brought back from the New World in the eighteenth century and the place that remains the heart of the *pimientos de Padrón* belt.

After we returned to New York, I would daydream about what that festival might have been like. In those dreams I see myself with an unlimited supply of *pimientos,* grown and cooked by the masters. I am drinking wine. I am eating octopus, of course. People keep bringing more *pimientos* to my table. Just before I leave, a stranger sits down. He speaks perfect English. He tells me that he's importing the seeds of *pimientos de Padrón* to America—returning them to their hemisphere of origin. He's an entrepreneur, of course, but his interest in *pimientos* is much broader than that: he views what he's doing as a sort of repatriation project. Oddly enough, he tells me, north-central New Jersey has precisely the same soil conditions as Herbón. He already has orders from Spanish restaurants in New York, a list of which he shows me. I glance at his list, noting that several of the restaurants are in my neighborhood. This man displays a wide knowledge of peppers, and he seems to be what my father would have called a real go-getter—someone who wouldn't hesitate to tackle any project. I ask him if he's familiar at all with Cajun boudin.

Before Alice and I left for our next visit to Galicia, ten years later, we confirmed that the *pimientos de Padrón* festival was definitely scheduled for the first Saturday of August. We arrived in Santiago a week before that. Why take a chance? Also, we intended to do some pepper research, not all of it at the table. I'd arranged to meet with Julio Martín, long the agricultural extension agent for an area that includes the patch of land around Padrón and Herbón. Señor Martín was not encouraging about the possibility of my being able to cross *pimientos de Padrón* off my Register of Frustration and Deprivation anytime soon. The peppers I yearn for, he said, amount to a relatively small crop produced on small family holdings— perhaps a hundred families have been granted numbers that they can put on their pepper bags signifying authentic *pimientos de Padrón*—and no export system has ever been put together. Thirty percent of the crop is consumed in Galicia, and virtually all of the rest is distributed to other parts of Spain. Given the fact that *pimientos de Padrón* are harvested in Galicia only in the summertime, Señor Martín told me, the innocent who has a plate of peppers at a Madrid tapas bar in January is actually eating a legume produced in southern Spain or even North Africa.

But we were in Galicia, in August, and we could eat the real article, sometimes three times a day. For a week, I watched myself living out pepper dreams. There we are eating *pimientos de Padrón* along with razor clams and Serrano ham in a *jamonería* (ham specialist) not far from the cathedral square in Santiago. We are eating peppers and cuttlefish and sardines at a table outside one of the restaurants lining a sort of alleyway in the graceful old quarter of Pontevedra. We are eating *pimientos de Padrón* and sardines in an outdoor café on the harbor of Barqueiro, a fishing village along the fjords known as the Rias Altas. In Lugo, we are eating peppers in one of those distinguished Spanish restaurants that line the walls with photographs of the celebrated who have dined there— including, in this case, the pope. The pope! There's no stopping us. Across the bay from Ferrol, in a fishing town called Mugardos, we are eating peppers in a *pulpería*—an octopus restaurant—along with *pulpo de Mugardesa,* a version of octopus served nowhere else. In bars, we're eating dollar-and-a-half plates of peppers, biting them off while holding them by the stem; in fancy restaurants, we're eating six-dollar-a-plate peppers, with their stems removed, presumably to encourage the customer to use a knife and fork. At times, I thought I could hear my mother saying, "Eat your vegetables!" Then I remembered something Julio Martín had told us: If *pimientos de Padrón* were allowed to stay on the vine, they would grow large and red and inappropriately spicy. We weren't just eating vegetables, I reminded Alice; we were eating baby vegetables.

Did we reach any critical conclusions? At times we had the feeling that peppers eaten some distance from Padrón tended to be less reliably marvelous, although, to be honest about it, I don't recall seeing any left on our plates. In Porto do Barqueiro, for instance, our peppers didn't seem quite as tasty as usual, although that could have been simply in comparison with the fat sardines that we had at the same time. In Betanzos, in a restaurant where the razor clams were stupendous, the number of spicy peppers seemed particularly high, leading me to speculate that there might be a little joke among *pimientos de Padrón* people to send the hot ones to Betanzos. On the other hand, in Lugo, an interior city where it was difficult to find authentic *pimientos de Padrón* in the city market, the peppers at lunch were excellent. With no certain pattern emerging, there was nothing to do but keep eating. Toward the end of the week, I used the calculator mode of my pocket-sized electronic Spanish-English dictionary to estimate that Alice and I had consumed about seven hundred peppers.

Julio Martín had kindly agreed to accompany us to the *pimientos de Padrón* festival. We were to meet across from the Padrón city market. It was a landmark we knew, since we had been there the previous Sunday to inspect the shellfish and to snack in one of the eating tents on barbecue pork ribs and octopus—the octopus snatched out of the bubbling water of a huge pot, then held on a wooden block and snipped into bite-sized pieces with a scissors, then doused with salt, paprika, and olive oil. (They don't pretty up octopus in Galicia. If you've always wondered whether those little suction-cup thingees might adhere to the tongue while you were trying to get them masticated, Galicia is the place to find out.) Three friends of ours, two from London and one from Paris, had arrived in Santiago to join us for the festival. Alice said she felt some echoes of *The Sun Also Rises*, when Jake Barnes and Lady Brett and that bunch went to the festival in Pamplona, except that this time the group was focused on tiny green peppers instead of bulls.

On Saturday morning, the rain was coming down in sheets. It occurred to me that our festival jinx might have held. The previous Sunday, we'd arrived at Isla de Arousa for the mussel festival only to discover that we were there a week early. The Viking festival at Catoira—a celebration that features the disembarkation of some reenactors with horns on their hats and then, I'd been told, a lot of octopus and other Viking grub—was so jammed with traffic that we'd turned tail without getting out of the car. The only festival we'd actually managed to attend was the little town of Laro's celebration of *tortillas*—which in Spain are flat, pie-shaped potato omelets. The *tortillas* were free, unless you count having to listen to an exceedingly long speech before they were distributed, and they were good *tortillas*. But townspeople, who arrived carrying baskets of foodstuffs to supplement the *tortillas* (and octopus) being offered on the grounds, had reserved all of the picnic tables, so we had to bolt our food before the true owners of our table arrived. Also, to be direct about it, I do not yearn for potato omelets.

Although it was possible that the entire pepper festival

would have to be suspended, Señor Martín remained calm. We all repaired to a bar called Casa Diós, which would be on the parade route if the rain lifted enough to permit the procession of farm implements that customarily moves out around noon to provide the festival's kickoff. As it turned out, the proprietors of the bar were pepper growers themselves—someone said that the grandmother, in her eighties, still went to the Santiago market every morning with her basket—so we asked for a couple of orders, along with a salt cod *empanada* and some sliced pork. The *pimientos de Padrón* were the best I'd ever tasted—soft, juicy, obviously snatched from the pot just before they turned brown. "I'm okay now," I said to Alice, "even if the rain doesn't stop."

But it did. There was still a strong drizzle as a line of tractors and plows pulling homemade floats—models of the original monastery in one case, three-foot-high peppers with arms in another—passed in front of the Casa Diós, but not long after that the sun came out. And not long after that, we were at the *pimientos de Padrón* festival. It was held in a sort of community picnic grounds out in the country, next to a graceful old convent that, I gathered, was on the site of where the Franciscans had their inspired stroke of agronomy centuries before. Peppers, in thick, shoulder-high plants that looked too dense to walk through, were visible in adjoining fields. In a little valley, picnic tables had been set out under gnarled oak trees. The tractors and plows from the procession were parked in front of the stage. Someone was selling octopus and barbecued pork. A mountain of *broa*, the dense cornmeal bread I'd always identified with Portugal, stood on a large table. Not far away, in three huge black pots suspended over an open fire, *pimientos de Padrón* were being fried in oil.

Before I knew what was happening, Señor Martín had pulled me up on the stage, where the mayor and other dignitaries were gathered to award parade trophies and do some speechifying. I hadn't noticed any other outsiders around, and I suppose he'd called me forward in the spirit that high school reunion organizers give a small prize to the person who's come the farthest. Alice and our friends were pointing to me on the stage and laughing; it was as if Jake Barnes had jumped into the bullring, tearing off his sport coat to use as a cape. Still, I thought about giving a little speech, and I patted my pocket to make sure the Spanish-English dictionary was in place. "You could say that I'm sort of a pilgrim myself," I might begin. But when the time came for me to be introduced, all I could muster was "*Muchas gracias.*" I wanted to get to the peppers.

After the ceremony, the mayor invited us to share his table. There was wine. There was, it almost goes without saying, octopus. There were *empanadas*. There was *broa*. People kept bringing more and more plates of peppers. Nobody came up to talk about a scheme to grow *pimientos de Padrón* in America, it's true, but I had four packets of seeds in my suitcase. An essay on *pimientos de Padrón* that I'd read in a book about eating in Galicia had reported rumors of success growing the peppers in California. I happen to have a friend in California who is adventurous in such matters. I had not given up.

When I got back from Galicia, I turned over the four packets of seeds to my friend in California, but the report of a

successful crop—a crop, I'd been thinking, that was so boun-
tiful it merited a festival of its own—never came. Occasionally, I would get vague reports of *pimiento de Padrón* sightings
at a farmers' market someplace out there. Once, I received a
letter from a woman who said that in New Jersey—where, not
that far from the place my imaginary acquaintance had chosen
as the scene of the pepper's repatriation to the Western Hemisphere, there happens to be a substantial Galician community—some of her relatives and their neighbors are obsessed
with raising *pimientos de Padrón* in their backyard gardens. She
invited me to join members of the community at a Galician
feast built around the crop of *pimientos*. Unfortunately, the
feast was in July, when I'm in Nova Scotia and have a reluctance to return to the United States which is somewhere
between a policy and an article of religious belief. The next
July found me back in Nova Scotia, wondering whether I'd
made a mistake in not being a bit more flexible about my travel
restrictions. Fortunately, I had Lunenburg sausage to soothe
my feelings. Also Lunenburg pudding—a completely different foodstuff that looks like a sausage but is ready to eat, usually on a cracker with drinks. I love Lunenburg pudding. I've
never seen Lunenburg pudding outside of Nova Scotia.

3

THE FRYING GAME

No, I do not believe it would be fair to say that for fifteen years I thought of nothing but the fried fish I ate on Baxters Road in 1986. That statement would be inaccurate even if you expanded it to include the chicken, also fried, that I ate on Baxters Road during the same week. I like to think of myself as a person who can go about his daily tasks without obsessing over a juicy piece of marlin encased in dark, spicy batter. What I am willing to admit is that making Baxters Road my dinner destination for a couple of nights in a row that year did have an impact on me. Whenever the subject of Caribbean vacations came up after that, I did not think of lying on a secluded beach or drinking some sort of rum concoction at a thatched-roof bar or luxuriating in a fabulously expensive resort or peering at outrageously colored fish that had assembled at a coral reef for my inspection. I thought instead of a dark

and rather run-down street in Bridgetown, the capital of Barbados—Baxters Road.

There I was at the top of the street, where a dozen women,
illuminated by the wood fires in the braziers in front of them,
fried fish in deep iron skillets. There I was sitting in a bar
named Enid's, half a block away, where a woman named
Shirley served me a plate of fried chicken that was destined to
secure her a place in my fried-chicken pantheon not far from
the late Chicken Betty Lucas, the great Kansas City pan fryer I
tried to get my old hometown to name a bridge after. There I
was watching Alice try Baxters Road fish for the first time. She
had ordered what people in other parts of the world call
dorado or mahimahi—a fish whose blunt head calls to mind
the mug of an unsuccessful prizefighter. Bajans (as Barbadians
are often called) refer to it as dolphin, and fry it in steaks. Alice
was taking a bite of the dolphin while standing right next to
the woman who had just fried it and put it in a brown paper
bag and handed it to us—as good a place as any to do the sampling, since there was nowhere to sit down. I later recorded
that moment: "Alice acknowledged that it was about the finest
piece of fried fish she had ever eaten. You could hear the
appreciation in her voice when she turned to the woman who
had sold it to us and said, 'What are these spices?' The woman
laughed. 'That's my little secret, dearie,' she said."

It would also be fair to say that my specific yearning for
Baxters Road fried fish has always been more intense than my
general yearning for the Caribbean. Deep into a New York
winter, my thoughts do turn southward now and then. I've
always thought of Caribbean vacation destinations as belonging in roughly two categories—Actual Places and Tropical

Isles. An Actual Place—Jamaica, say, or Martinique or Puerto Rico—has the characteristics of a small country, such as a multifaceted economy and a real city and authentic traffic jams. In an Actual Place, you tend to rent an air-conditioned sedan rather than an open beach buggy, the car of choice on a Tropical Isle. My problem on a Caribbean vacation, I think, is that I'm never completely confident that the right category has been chosen. In the bustle of an Actual Place, my thoughts sometimes wander to the joys of those quiet and picturesque islands where you know that absolutely nothing exciting is going to happen to you once you've settled down from the dramatic landing on a pockmarked little airstrip. But when I'm on a Tropical Isle, I think of the advantages of an Actual Place—especially at mealtime.

What you eat on a Tropical Isle in the Caribbean tends to be brought in from somewhere else, and the most creative chef might not be creative enough to overcome the extended stopover that had to be made in St. Thomas or San Juan while the waybill problem was being sorted out. An Actual Place may have a cuisine of its own. At the least, it has the capacity to grow a head of lettuce. It is likely to have a fishery and a serious farmers' market and some specialties whose ties to the local culture are stronger than those that can be claimed for, say, pasta primavera or Buffalo chicken wings.

Barbados, the most densely populated country in the Western Hemisphere, is definitely an Actual Place. A lot of it resembles the unzoned outskirts of a rather large city—although there are also vast sugarcane fields and some spectacular beaches and a lot of estates inhabited in the winter by enormously rich people from England and America. It has a substantial history and a legislature of ancient vintage. Some would say that it has its own language: the island accent shades into a patois that is often called Bajan, musical to the ear and sometimes difficult for a foreigner to understand. Once, at a stand at the Cheapside Market in Bridgetown, I asked about a vaguely familiar fried object next to the fish cakes, and the pleasant young woman in charge said something that sounded like "jaahm steak." For some reason, what ran through my mind was jumbo, an old Pittsburgh word for bologna, but I ordered one anyway. As the young woman handed it to me, I asked her how it was spelled, and she began "d-r-u . . ." I took a closer look. No wonder it had seemed familiar. It was a drumstick. Even if you understand the words you might not get the meaning, since you're unlikely to know that, say, "bulljoe" means "salt cod" and you may not catch the drift of a proverb like (to quote from *Bajan Proverbs* by Margot Blackman) "Calabash button suit crocus bag trousers."

Barbados also has a strong local specialty: fish. The flying fish—a small, silver creature found in great schools that take occasional orchestrated leaps out of the water—is essentially the icon of the country, used in mottoes and logos in the way Americans use the bald eagle. Even though a flying fish is not much larger than a sardine, Bajans customarily butterfly it. Then they fry it, and often put it in a round roll to make the sort of sandwich they call a cutter—dressed with coleslaw or salad or the mustard-based pepper sauce that Bajans are referring to when they say "You want pepper?" (The bald eagle may be more majestic, but just try making a palatable sandwich out of it.) As the freeze clung to New York one winter, fifteen years after Alice and I took that first trip to Barbados, I thought of flying fish. I also thought of dolphin and marlin and swordfish and tuna and kingfish. I thought of Enid's fried chicken. In my thoughts, they were all sizzling in a deep skillet on Baxters Road. We made arrangements to go to Barbados. The Tropical Isle would have to wait.

How would I describe my response to being told that Baxters Road was no longer the preferred spot in Barbados for eating fried fish? *Wary* is the word that leaps to mind. Nobody was claiming that the fish fryers had abandoned their positions on Baxters Road. Instead, we were being told that in recent years it had become customary for both tourists and Bajans to patronize a collection of fish fryers gathered at a fishing port called Oistins, on the south coast, and that Baxters Road had, in the meantime, become what the concierge at the hotel called "a bit rowdy." I remembered Baxters Road as being on the ragged side of raffish even in 1986. Its commercial establishments ran heavily to bars that, particularly late on a weekend evening, were patronized by Bajans in a celebratory mood. Given the bar crowds and the fish fryers and the ramshackle buildings, I had written in 1986, arriving at Baxters Road was a bit like wandering onto the set of *Porgy and Bess*.

What made me wary was that Oistins sounded suspiciously like a cleaned-up version of Baxters Road, the culinary equivalent of those tidy programs of native ceremonies that a hotel in the South Pacific might put together for the entertainment of elderly Americans visiting on package tours. Barbados itself has long had restaurants where you can find the local specialties conveniently packaged in what is sometimes called a Bajan buffet—the pickled pumpkin and the marinated green bananas and the pepperpot labeled as carefully as the specimens at the local botanical garden. In any number of places at any number of times, I have resisted suggestions that I might have a more enjoyable meal in a somewhat better neighborhood. For years, travelers who had returned from visiting Kansas City told me about asking their host to take them to Arthur Bryant's, the barbecue shrine, and being told that they didn't really want to go to that place in that neighborhood. One of those travelers told of being taken instead to the club at the baseball stadium, where he was served what the menu described as "a fish of the Pacific waters"; the next night, he liberated himself from the locals, like a Russian ballet dancer in Cold War days shaking his KGB minders, and took a cab to Bryant's. Surroundings that seem modest, or maybe even dangerous, happen to be natural to both fried chicken and fried fish. My last taste of chicken fried by Chicken Betty Lucas—the nonpareil—was at the coffee shop of the Metro Auto Auction in Lee's Summit, Missouri. On our second night in Barbados, a Tuesday, Alice and I headed for Baxters Road.

I had to admit that it appeared somewhat the worse for wear. Several of the business establishments were shuttered. A couple of people were sleeping on the sidewalk. Although there were two conventional supermarkets, two or three other stores were arranged in a way that put both the merchandise and the salesclerk within what amounted to a cage. Enid's, to my monumental sadness, no longer existed. But, even though we had arrived early in the week and early in the evening, there were four or five fish fryers in the usual spot. In fact, a couple of them had stalls that seemed much more elaborate than I remembered, and the fish was being served not in paper bags but in polystyrene containers with hinged covers, accompanied by plastic forks and paper napkins. The amenities of Baxters Road still didn't include any place to sit.

We bought some fried tuna from a stand called Sandra's, and walked a few yards away to eat in the light emerging from the Pink Star, a bar that was offering liver cutters as a special that night. The tuna came with what's called in Barbados macaroni pie. Somehow, I had forgotten about Bajan macaroni pie. It looks like traditional macaroni and cheese, served in a pale loaf that's shaped like a generous helping of lasagna, but, like Bajan fish cakes or Bajan fried fish, it's likely to be slightly spicy even before it's doused with pepper sauce. It tastes, in other words, like macaroni and cheese made by your mother on a day she had a little devilment in her, the source of which was probably not the sort of thing she would reveal to the children.

Sandra put out an acceptable version of macaroni pie— a cheering reminder of all the side dishes to come. Sandra's tuna was simply magnificent. The fish itself was moist and flavorful. The batter was thin, with no resemblance at all to what Chicken Betty used to refer to contemptuously as plaster-cast batter. From what I've read, I assume it included lime and pepper and chives and ginger and cloves; we were not inclined to pause for an analysis of what Sandra's little secret was. Fortunately, we had two plastic forks with the one order of tuna. Fried tuna! I envisioned people across the United States ordering tuna in those trendy joints I think of as sleepy-time restaurants, where everything is served on a bed of something else. The waiter is informing them, in a slightly patronizing tone, that the tuna is seared and absolutely always served pink in the middle, on a bed of lentils. I felt sorry for those people, even though they presumably didn't have to eat standing up.

I had no intention of rejecting the Oistins fish fry out of hand. In fact, I was looking forward to it, particularly after a wide-ranging discussion of the fish-eating landscape with two Bajan men who had been shooting the breeze at a closed filling station in Bridgetown when we stopped to ask directions to Baxters Road. Their enthusiasm for an establishment at Oistins called the Fish Net, which grills rather than fries its fish, was among some strong indications I'd received that the Oistins fish feed could not be dismissed as a sanitized mock-up of the real article. We had already arranged to go on the next Friday with some friends who happened to be on the island. Although it's possible to find fish at Oistins just about every night, the operation goes into high gear on the weekends, particularly Friday nights. We were already armed not only with instructions from the filling station kibitzers but also with a crude map of the Oistins fish stalls, provided by a friend in New York who had described the grilled marlin at one stall as a transformational experience.

In the days we waited for the Oistins fish fry, I began to develop an improbable craving for macaroni pie shortly after breakfast every morning—a craving that the Freudians would presumably trace to having been brought up by someone who early on ceded her macaroni and cheese responsibilities to the Kraft corporation. One morning, late in the week, I held out until almost eleven before I bought my first helping of macaroni pie, and found myself boasting to Alice about my willpower.

Once I had my macaroni pie fix, I was usually ready for a cutter. I had flying-fish cutters everywhere from the expensive hotels on the West Coast to the bars and beach restaurants on the windy and sparsely populated and breathtakingly beautiful East Coast. I had stewed salt-fish cutters and fish-cake cutters. Given the dough content of a Bajan fish cake, a fish-cake cutter could be thought of as something approaching a bread sandwich, an observation I offer without a trace of criticism. (At a place called Sweet-n-Tart Cafe, in Manhattan's Chinatown, my daughter Abigail and I love to eat something that's on the menu as "Fried Dough with Rice Noodle"—a cylindrical roll of the sort New Yorkers call a cruller wrapped in a large noodle. Like a Bajan fish-cake cutter, it's particularly welcome on days when you're worried that you might not have gotten in your daily allotment of starch.)

Along the way, I tried other Bajan specialties. I had what Bajans call pudding and souse, or at least the pudding half; souse does not have the appearance of something that is obviously edible. I had breadfruit chips. I had peas and rice. I had roti. At one of the food booths at the annual Holetown Festival, I asked for cou-cou, which I remembered vaguely as a sort of cornmeal pudding, accompanied by seacat, a dish I'd never heard of and couldn't picture from the description offered in a strong Bajan accent by the person who took my order. While I was waiting for my plate of cou-cou and seacat to arrive, it began to occur to me that I might be unable to tell which was which. That turned out not to be a problem: the cou-cou was the one that had no resemblance at all to a cat. It was delicious. I passed up the seacat, just in case its name turned out to be one of those rare examples of the normally metaphorical Bajan dialect being woodenly literal.

Although Oistins is indeed a fishing port, there is nothing picturesque about it. The fish market is an open building of concrete that was put up by the government. Across a busy road there are stores that amount to a strip mall. Next to the fish market, a long parking lot between the beach and the road has maybe twenty fish stalls and a couple of bars and dozens of picnic tables. The stalls have names like Dora's Fish Corner and Fay's Strictly Bajan Cooking and Taste de Rainbow and Angel's de Grill Fish Corner—the last two not attempts at French but nods toward the down-home, since *the* sounds like *de* in the dialect. We arrived early on Friday evening, around seven o'clock, but there were already hundreds of people there. Most of them appeared to be tourists; apparently, Bajans tend to show up later in the evening. At least two sound systems were blaring different songs, and some people had started to dance, in one of the bars and outside. There was, I was relieved to find, nothing at all tidy about Oistins.

The line for grilled fish at the Fish Net was already long. Alice volunteered to stand in it, another one of our group staked out a picnic table, and the rest of us split up to acquire whatever else we needed—some fish cakes for hors d'oeuvres and several bottles of Banks, the local beer, and a couple of orders of macaroni pie and some grilled marlin at the booth we figured our New York friend, who does not have a future as a cartographer, may have been trying to indicate on his map. I also got some fried dolphin at Dora's Fish Corner, just in case. When Alice finally got served, it took three or four people to help her carry all of the fish to our table. She'd gotten marlin, dolphin, shark, tuna, and swordfish—all of it just off the grill.

The grilled fish was excellent, but once we started passing it around, the conversation sounded something like this:

"This marlin is the best," Rob said. "It's fantastic."

"I think that's the swordfish you're eating," Em said.

"No," John said, pointing at his plate. "This is the swordfish."

"That's the shark," Alice said. "The shark is great. Unless that's the marlin."

I liked it all, but I found myself returning again and again to the fried dolphin. Could it be, I asked Alice, that fried fish is simply better than grilled fish? Alice said that the frying did indeed seem to seal in the fish's moisture and flavor. That sounded right. Otherwise, I'd have to face the possibility that what I'd been yearning for all those years was not the fish but the batter.

The fried dolphin confirmed what had been dawning on me during the previous days: fish doesn't have to be fried right on Baxters Road to be spectacular. During the week leading up to our Oistins pig-out, I'd eaten excellent fried fish at a couple of church dinners and at the Holetown Festival and at a stand at Six Men's Bay, where hawkers line a narrow strip of ground between the road and the beach to sell flying fish in lots of fifty or a hundred. In fact, it occurred to me, since vendors on the streets of New York prepare Italian sausages and taro cakes and *tacos al carbón* right in front of your eyes, why not fried fish?

There happens to be a substantial Bajan community in Brooklyn. On mild evenings, the cousins of Sandra and Dora and Fay could easily cross over to Manhattan—say, to the strip of land where a bike path runs along the Hudson River, just a few blocks from where I live in Greenwich Village— and set up stands with names like De Flatbush Corner.

For me, of course, their fish would be neighborhood take- out. I can imagine strolling over there on a spring evening to pick up dinner. As I approach the stands, which are in the flickering light of the braziers and the headlights from West Street, I hear somebody say, *"Buenas noches."* It's the Galician go-getter I'd imagined meeting at the *pimientos de Padrón* fes- tival we missed years ago. He's taking a break from New Jer- sey pepper planting, and, as someone genetically programmed for seafood eating, he can't resist the fish prepared by the Bajans from Brooklyn.

The go-getter insists that we share an hors d'oeuvre, an order of Bajan fish cakes he has just picked up, while he fills me in on his efforts to bring *pimientos de Padrón* back to their home hemisphere. The project is going quite well, he tells me. In fact, some modern American agricultural techniques have accelerated the process of bringing the peppers to maturation. He expects to have a harvest in June—in plenty of time for a feast before I leave for Nova Scotia. Greatly heartened by that news, I suggest that as long as we're at it, we share just one helping of macaroni pie. He agrees, and asks if, by chance, I happen to know what the proprietor of De Flatbush Corner puts in her fish batter.

4.

MAGIC SANDWICH

—
—

In the scene that I replayed in my mind for many years, I'm
standing in a market in Nice. (Yes, I realize that in many of the
scenes that I replay in my mind I am standing in a market
somewhere; I have no control over that.) In this case, I'm in
the produce and flower market that runs down the center of
the Cours Saleya six days a week. The Cours Saleya is an
elongated plaza that's used as a sort of pedestrian boulevard in
Old Nice, just inland from Nice's world-famous beach—
a wide strip of jagged stones that an American accustomed to
the great sandy edges of Long Island or Southern California
might at first mistake for an unpaved parking lot that happens
to have an ocean next to it. In the scene, it's 1983. Our family
is staying in a house in Tourrettes-sur-Loup, not far away;
this is before our daughters, oblivious of my efforts to locate
some process that would freeze them at an age that made it
appropriate for them to remain under my roof, simply went

ahead and grew up. Feeling a twinge of hunger late in the morning—being in a market, particularly a market anywhere near the Mediterranean, tends to do that to me—I step up to a serving window over a display case and ask for a *pan bagnat*.

The woman behind the case reaches in and withdraws a sandwich. It's on a circular bun that looks large enough to accommodate the sort of outsized hamburger you might fashion for Popeye's friend Wimpy—who, I might as well admit, was a boyhood hero of mine in an era when other lads were gaga over Batman or Captain Marvel. She removes the top of the bun, revealing a damp mélange of tuna fish and chopped onions and lettuce and tomatoes and olives and hard-boiled eggs. She pours on some olive oil, presumably to make up for whatever might have evaporated since she prepared the sandwich earlier that morning. She hands the sandwich over the counter. I pay her and take the first bite before I've moved an inch. I turn to Alice. "If I could speak French, I would say *Mon Dieu!*" I tell her. But even as I work my way through the huge sandwich, it begins to dawn on me that leaving the Nice area will mean giving up *pan bagnats;* I have never eaten one anywhere else. I can see myself adding them to the list of favorite dishes that never seem to appear outside their place of origin—the Register of Frustration and Deprivation.

I am momentarily saddened, but then it occurs to me that a *pan bagnat* is not something that requires rare ingredients or some special oven; we're essentially talking here about a tuna-fish sandwich. How long could it be before the *pan bagnat* catches on in America? (After all, this vision takes place in 1983, at a time when a previously unknown Italian bread or a previously unknown Chinese provincial cuisine seemed to sweep over Manhattan every week.) As I finish the last bite and begin to deal with the olive oil stains on my shirt, I am buoyed by the thought that the sort of New York joints that once went from being totally squidless to being buried in fried calamari will soon have *pan bagnat* as a familiar menu item. Having to go to Nice to get a *pan bagnat* will be told as a tale from the Model T days of preglobalized eating, when you had to go to Italy for sun-dried tomatoes and couldn't find sourdough bread outside the confines of San Francisco.

Wrong. The day came when I realized that I hadn't had a *pan bagnat* in seventeen years. I can't imagine why sandwiches, which seem eminently transportable, are so often tethered to their place of origin. I have never seen an Italian beef sandwich outside of Chicago or a beef-on-weck outside of Buffalo—although I was once told that homesick Buffalonians who have settled in the vicinity of Hollywood, Florida, hold a beef-on-weck banquet every winter to stave off melancholy. The tension of which sandwich to have on a short stopover in New Orleans—an oyster loaf at Casamento's, a muffuletta at the Central Grocery, a Ferdi's special at Mother's, a shrimp po'boy at Uglesich's—is intensified by the certain knowledge that you're not going to get the precise match of any of them outside of Louisiana. A similar cloud of anticipated deprivation hangs over the sunny pleasure of eating four or five barely cooked scallops on a hamburger bun, with tartar sauce and lettuce and tomato, at the Innlet Cafe in Mahone Bay, Nova Scotia, the only place in my experience where this simple delight is available.

Finally, as the century waned, I spotted *pan bagnat* listed on the lunch menu of a pleasant-looking bistro not far from where I live—the first time I'd seen it mentioned in New York.

Naturally, I stopped in. The sandwich I was given was a cooked patty on a square bun—what I would call a tunaburger. "I don't crave a take on a *pan bagnat*," I told Alice. "I don't crave a statement on the *pan bagnat* theme. I do not crave an interpretation of a *pan bagnat* or an Asian fusion version of a *pan bagnat*. I crave a *pan bagnat*. We'd better go to Nice."

"This is not exactly what I had in mind," I said to Alice. I had taken a couple of bites from a *pan bagnat* and had yet to reach what I believe rocket scientists call the payload. The bread was dry, even after the last-minute spray of olive oil. I inspected the small mound of tuna and fixings that formed an island in the middle of the vast whiteness of the lower bun. I suppose you have to admire the enterprise of someone who, at the height of the tomato season in the South of France, manages to find the precise equivalent of those American supermarket tomatoes that have the same shelf life as a can of cleanser, but I was reminded of the phrase a serious eater I know in Paris had used to describe a run-of-the-mill *pan bagnat:* "yesterday's salade Niçoise on a bun." This *pan bagnat* had been handed to me through a window over a display case—perhaps not precisely the same window as in 1983, but, still, a window on the Cours Saleya in Nice. It seemed to constitute disquieting evidence that some of the people I'd talked to before leaving New York were correct in saying that it's becoming difficult to put your hands on a decent *pan bagnat* even in the heart of Nice. I tried to remain calm.

I was helped in that endeavor by a large can of olive oil. It was on our table at a restaurant we stopped in for lunch just after

I had the inferior *pan bagnat* as a sort of hors d'oeuvre. This was not the discreet little saucer of olive oil that a Tuscan trattoria in Houston or Minneapolis might bring to the table these days in case you want something to dip your bread in. This was a serious can of olive oil from a local maker—a beautiful cylinder in blue, with gold stars on it. It reminded me of the large pitcher of schmaltz—liquid chicken fat—that the Parkway, a Rumanian Jewish restaurant on the Lower East Side, used to place on its tables for the convenience of customers who felt the need to improve on the chef's excesses. Among the other theories offered for why I so look forward to eating in just about any modest bistro near the Mediterranean and can contain my enthusiasm for eating in three-star restaurants in Paris is the theory that I have a limited tolerance of butter and an unlimited tolerance of olive oil. The can in the middle of our table told me that I was in the olive oil zone of influence. I was in a city that as late as 1860 had still been part of Italy. I was sitting a matter of yards from the Mediterranean. I was in a place whose specialties include some of my favorite foods—*pissaladière* and sardines and ratatouille. I had not yet even tasted what some people think is the truly great market dish of Nice—*socca,* a thin pancake, not much thicker than a crepe, made of nothing but chickpea flour, water, olive oil, and salt and pepper. I felt optimistic that I would find a superior *pan bagnat;* even if I didn't, I wouldn't go hungry. I ordered some grilled sardines and pulled the olive oil toward my end of the table, just in case they needed improving.

To help search out quality *pan bagnats,* I had assembled a small team that included Lydie Marshall, a noted cooking teacher and cookbook writer who used to live in New York and now holds her classes in a château that she and her husband have restored in Nyons, a few hours northwest of Nice. Lydie had brought with her a sort of *pan bagnat* treasure map drawn by a friend of hers named Bruno, a landscape designer, and when we gathered the next morning to plan our first foray, she spread it out before us. It showed the shorefront promenade and inland boulevard that form the borders of Old Nice, and, between them, a rather detailed drawing of an intersection. Just which intersection, of the dozens of intersections in Old Nice, was not indicated.

"If this is Bruno's idea of perspective, I'd like to see one of his gardens," I said.

Lydie said Bruno was a brilliant designer and a serious eater. "He says that this is the place where everyone goes for *pan bagnats,*" she said, tapping the drawing of the intersection with her finger.

As I was about to make another disparaging remark about Bruno, I suddenly recognized the intersection. I had been there on an early morning walk a couple of hours before; it was obviously the end of a one-block street called Miralheti that juts down into Old Nice from Boulevard Jean Jaure. I remembered seeing the tables and stools Bruno had drawn in the street, between a bar called René Socca and a place with two outdoor serving windows over display cases of Niçoise specialties. Fifteen minutes later, we were sitting at one of the tables with half a dozen empty plates in front of us, and I was saying that, upon some reconsideration, I had decided that Bruno was a man of considerable sagacity.

Yes, I'd just had the sort of *pan bagnat* I hadn't eaten since 1983. But I'd also been wowed by the other Niçoise specialties.

We'd had sardine beignets. We'd had *pissaladière* that had a fine crust and caramelized onions good enough to make you forget the crust. We'd had at least two orders of *socca*, and only the certain knowledge that we were going to have to eat lunch in about an hour kept me from going to the window to get more. We'd also had a dish that consisted of fresh sardines split and then topped with a sort of paste made mostly of what the French call *blette* and we call Swiss chard. (What people in New Orleans do with oysters and spinach to create oysters Rockefeller is simply a tonier version of what people in Nice do with sardines and Swiss chard—a piece of evidence to support A. J. Liebling's theory that New Orleans is essentially a Mediterranean city.) All in all, I was so impressed that I could hardly wait for lunch.

A friend of Lydie's who lives in Nice had arranged a lunchtime interview with Thérésa, a purveyor of *socca* and *pan bagnat* and other Niçoise specialties in the Cours Saleya market. In general, what would be the median strip if the Cours Saleya were a conventional boulevard is reserved for market stalls—except on Mondays, when it becomes antiques stalls, and evenings, when it's transformed into extra tables for the restaurants and cafés that run along what would be the curbsides. But amidst the stalls of vendors selling fruits and vegetables and olives and spices and special Niçoise sweets in the middle of the Cours Saleya, Thérésa stands behind what looks like one of those barrels that down-and-outers sometimes build a fire in to give themselves a little warmth on chilly nights. The barrel has a charcoal fire in it, used to keep the *socca* on top of it warm. *Socca* is made in a very shallow circular pan, about three times the diameter of an extra-large-family-size-pig-out-special pizza—a pan that fits precisely on Thérésa's barrel. Since the twenties, Chez Thérésa's *socca* has been made in a wood-burning oven a couple of blocks from the market. It's transported to the barrel on a specially designed cart that's pulled on a motorbike by a man named Robert, who is, as far as I know, the only person on earth who can accurately describe his occupation as *socca* schlepper.

Behind Thérésa and her barrel, there are a few tables, which she somehow serves while handing out helpings of *socca* and *pissaladière* and *tourte aux blettes* and, of course, *pan bagnats* to those who prefer eating on the stroll. Thérésa herself is a handsome middle-aged woman, brassy in the way women who preside over market stalls often are. She wears tight clothes and huge gold earrings and is sometimes described as Felliniesque. She has become a sort of Niçoise icon—a symbol of the market and Old Nice and the deeply traditional Niçoise dishes. As soon as she found time to join us at one of the tables, she said that she was the third Thérésa, that her real name is Suzy, that she is half Jewish and half Spanish, and that her lengthiest commercial experience before she bought the operation from the second Thérésa, twelve years before, was in the clothing business in Israel. "I make the best *pan bagnat* in Nice," she said, in the same tone a Louisiana chef had once told me that after I tasted his étouffée I'd throw rocks at other people's étouffées, "and I'm not even Niçoise."

Could she be right? If the world were consistent, you might expect the most photographed and colorful vendor in the Nice market to produce a *pan bagnat* that could impress only a tourist whose sandwich eating normally did not stray beyond his suburb's fast-food double lane. But the world is not consistent. Years ago, when I was looking into a shortage of Dungeness crabs in San Francisco, I'd been surprised to discover that the only people who were almost certain to have fresh crabs just trucked in from Eureka were those colorful and often photographed characters manning the pots on Fisherman's Wharf.

Among the purveyors of *pan bagnats* in Nice—the bakeries and cafés and take-out places—Thérésa is one of the few I found who understands that the word *overstuffed* when applied to sandwiches is a compliment. She takes great care marinating the onions with olive oil and red wine vinegar and black pepper—a mixture she allows to stand overnight. She uses bread baked in a wood-burning oven. On my third or fourth visit to Chez Thérésa for a *pan bagnat*, I decided that even if what I was eating didn't make me want to throw rocks at absolutely every other *pan bagnat* served in Nice—the one at what we'd started calling Bruno's place or the one at a bar near the market called Chez Antoine—it was as good as *pan bagnats* get. I would have cleaned my plate if I'd had one.

I had never thought of Swiss chard as a staple of Niçoise cuisine. Actually, I hadn't done a lot of thinking about Swiss chard in any context. But as our team searched out Niçoise specialties, trying a plate of stuffed vegetables here and a zucchini *tourte* there and a grilled fresh anchovy somewhere else, Swiss chard seemed to pop up at odd times—during dessert, for instance, since *tourte aux blette* is made not only in savory form but in a terrific sweet version that has pignons and honey. I often found myself muttering *blette,* a word that can sound like an imitation of a small animal. *"Blette, blette,"* I'd say. "We are in the presence of *blette.*" The pâté maison at a restaurant called Les Arcades, in the pottery village of Biot, near Nice, had an unusual and satisfying taste. *"Blette,"* I said. *"Blette, blette."* At a place called Restaurant Simon, on the outskirts of the city, we had a stupendous version of the traditional Niçoise ravioli, made with *daube* (stewed beef) and Swiss chard. I wanted to ask Alice whether Simon's ravioli eaten with a side dish of its gnocchi (covered with the same sauce) would be considered a balanced meal, but all I could say was *"Blette."* When we had finished our first meal at a tiny restaurant near the Cours Saleya called La Mérenda and immediately made reservations for our second meal, we asked the waiter to reserve us some stuffed sardines, which they'd been out of, because it didn't take a genius to know what they'd be stuffed with.

The proprietor of La Mérenda, an informal little place with no phone and no credit cards but also no attitude, turned out to be Dominique Le Stanc, who had previously been at Chantecler, the two-star restaurant at the Hôtel Negresco. At our first La Mérenda meal, we'd had, among other things, a ratatouille that was so much better than any other ratatouille I'd ever eaten that it seemed to be a different dish and a *pistou* soup that brought to mind the days when Lydie Marshall was still our neighbor in the Village and made us *pistou* every autumn as soon as the cranberry beans began appearing at Union Square market. The stuffed sardines were everything we'd hoped for. *"Blette! Blette! Blette!"* I said, after I polished mine off and reached over to Alice's plate for another taste test, just to be sure. If France permitted those American-style city limits signs rather than the uniform signs that mark the city limits of every village and city in the country, I thought, the one announcing Nice might say, WELCOME TO NICE— SWISS CHARD CAPITAL OF THE WORLD.

Unless it said SOCCA CAPITAL OF THE WORLD. On our last evening in Nice, after the rest of the team had left, Alice and I went to Chez Pipo, a sort of corner tavern near the port. Pipo's food menu lists only four or five items. One was a delicious *pissaladière* with an almost sweet crust—a crust that made you think that some dear old granny nearby had been preparing the crust for an apple pie, in the loving way she'd gone about it for forty or fifty years, when someone rushed into her kitchen and snatched it away, muttering, "Pipo needs this." Another was the best *socca* we'd had in Nice. In Pipo's hands, a pancake that is almost too thin to be measured somehow has a soft inside, a crisp bottom, and a top that is done to the point at which it almost blisters. SOCCA CAP- ITAL OF THE WORLD would be appropriate, but, then, Nice could also be the stuffed sardine capital or the *daube* and *blette* ravioli capital, not to speak of the *pan bagnat* capital. It occurred to me that I had never had any of those dishes out- side of Nice, and that one result of our trip to Nice was the necessity of adding more items to the Register of Frustration and Deprivation that so often tormented me. Pouring each of us another glass of rosé, I asked the waitress for another order of *socca*, just to cheer myself up.

5

DESPERATELY SEEKING CEVICHE

On a steamy afternoon during a particularly hot June in New York, I was standing just off a curb in midtown Manhattan, trying unsuccessfully to get a cab to La Guardia Airport. I found myself having thoughts about the city which would not have pleased the Convention and Visitors Bureau—thoughts about the weather, thoughts about the structural flaws of the New York taxi industry. Then, still with no free taxis in sight, a Lincoln Town Car appeared in front of me. The uniformed driver lowered the window, and I was hit with frigid air. "Where you going?" he said.

"La Guardia," I said.

"Twenty-five dollars."

"Deal."

I got in. The driver identified himself as José. As we made it over the bridge and hit the Grand Central Parkway, he told me that he was from Ecuador, a country I had visited a few months before. I told him how much I'd enjoyed Ecuador—the gorgeous mountains, the markets, the climate that some have described as eternal spring, and, most of all, the ceviche.

Ceviche in Ecuador, I said, is to American ceviche what the seafood cocktails of Veracruz—oysters, shrimp, snails, octopus, crab, avocado, onions, and coriander chopped in front of your eyes into a liquid that in a just world would be what Bloody Mary mix tastes like—are to those balsa-wood and ketchup combinations that people in country club dining rooms get when they order the shrimp cocktail appetizer. (When I visited Veracruz with Abigail, she noticed that the purveyor of a particularly complicated seafood cocktail called *Vuelve a la Vida,* or Return to Life, described its curative powers in almost precisely the same terms as were used by a man who went from table to table in the outdoor cafés of the central square, offering a shock from a contraption that looked alarmingly like jumper cables. They could both be right.) Ecuadorian ceviche starts out with fresh fish cured by being marinated in lemon juice and enlivened by whatever else the chef has thought to add. It's liquid, like a bowl of tangy cold soup. Roasted corn kernels (flicked off Andean corn, whose kernels are sometimes the size of broad beans) are served on the side, to be tossed in for both flavor and crunch. Some restaurants offer as accompaniment not only roasted corn kernels but popcorn. Yes, popcorn—what less fortunate humans eat at the movies!

"You like that ceviche?" José asked. He sounded pleased, but mildly surprised, like an artist who has just heard effusive praise of a painting that is actually one of his earlier works.

"I love that ceviche, José," I said. "I would probably kill for that ceviche."

"When's your plane?" José asked.

"Oh, I've got time," I said. I had left myself a buffer for finding a taxi and grumbling about the city.

Instantly, he swerved off the Grand Central, and we were driving along a commercial street in Queens. Most of the signs on the stores were in Spanish. Some were in Chinese or Korean. In five minutes, we turned onto a side street, in front of a restaurant called Islas Galápagos.

We asked for two orders of ceviche. I ordered a cold Ecuadorian beer. We cleaned our bowls. Then we got back into the car and drove to La Guardia. "This is a great city, José," I said, as I hauled my baggage out of the icy splendor of his Town Car. "A little hot sometimes, but a great city."

On the other hand, the sort of New Yorker who's confident that even a stroke of good fortune can be complained about might point out that I had to go all the way to Queens to find Ecuadorian ceviche. At the time I met José, I'd almost never had a ceviche close to home. In New York, I had never even seen roasted corn kernels—what Ecuadorians sometimes call *tostados* and Peruvians call *cancha*. (They are neither roasted nor toasted, of course, but pan-fried, then salted, so that they're crunchy on the outside and soft, almost powdery, on the inside.) A couple of ceviches I'd had in Manhattan actually came accompanied by commercial Cornnuts, which, being approximately the right size and color, serve as a substitute for *cancha* about as effectively as marshmallows, being approximately the right size and color, would serve as a substitute for fresh Nova Scotia scallops.

Eventually, ceviche became more widely available in Manhattan. Around the time of my La Guardia adventure, Douglas Rodriguez brought it into the mainstream at Patria, and he later installed an entire ceviche bar at Chicama, complete with popcorn. I've even read about a Manhattan restaurant that offers a sort of *pour la table* ceviche appetizer for fifty dollars—an amount of money that in Ecuador would buy you enough ceviche to pickle your innards. Still, as the years passed, I thought more and more about another trip to serious ceviche country—which could mean, of course, almost anywhere in Latin America. When FBI agents tapped the prison phone calls of the former Panamanian dictator Manuel Noriega, one conversation that made them suspect that he was employing a devilishly clever code concerned a ceviche recipe. Ceviche is entrenched in Mexico; Rick Bayless, a scholar of Mexican food, has been serving it, usually made from marlin, since he opened Frontera Grill in Chicago in 1986. There is wide agreement, though, that the red-hot center of ceviche eating is around Ecuador and Peru—two countries that, after several decades, more or less settled their border dispute but continued to argue about who does the best job with marinated fish.

About five years after that serendipitous journey to La Guardia with José, I decided I had to go to Ecuador and Peru to get a booster shot of the real article. A number of people asked me if I really intended to travel all that way just to eat

ceviche. Not at all. In Peru, for instance, I was looking forward to sampling the stuffed pepper that many consider the
signature dish of Arequipa, and I fully intended to have my
share of Andean potatoes. I thought I might tuck away some
churros—possibly some *churros* with chocolate on them. I still
remembered a couple of the soups I'd had during my first trip
to Ecuador while staying at a charming inn called Hacienda
Cusin, near the great Andean market town of Otavalo, and I
thought I might see about arranging a reprise. I was seriously
considering guinea pig, which is such a strong regional specialty around Cuzco that the most famous seventeenth-century
religious painting in the Cuzco cathedral shows it as what
Jesus and his disciples are about to eat at the Last Supper. I
also had visions of sitting in a comfortable hotel bar somewhere sipping pisco sours while tossing down handfuls of *cancha* and expressing sympathy for travelers who were at that
moment at other hotel bars all around the world trying to
make do with mixed nuts. No, I assured the people question-
ing my trip, I wasn't going all that way just to eat ceviche. I
like to think of myself as a broad-gauged person.

Abigail, who persisted in living in San Francisco, agreed to
meet me in Peru, and Alice said she'd link up with us in Quito.
When I dropped into Chicama to ask Douglas Rodriguez for
some tips about where to eat down there, he said he'd prefer
to show us himself—actually, what he did was to get himself
so worked up with a description of the ceviche available in
an Ecuadorian seaside town called Salinas that he suddenly
shouted, "I'm going with you!"—and we arranged to meet
him and his wife and his publisher and the ceviche-bar chef

from Chicama in Guayaquil for a couple of days of sampling. We had become the ceviche gang.

"Would it be fair to say that you're wimping out on the guinea pig?" Abigail asked.

It occurred to me that this was one of those moments in the relationship between a parent and a grown child when it behooved the parent to say, in a considered tone, "Listen, kid, you're talking to someone who changed your diapers." We were in a restaurant in Cuzco. At the table next to us, there was a woman who had the appearance of a classic *gringa*— a very pale American of the type that the people of Cuzco sometimes refer to as a *cruda,* meaning, literally, "uncooked." She looked like the sort of tourist who might ask the waiter if there was anything available from a can, but we had just seen her presented with an entire roasted guinea pig, head and all. Abigail had spoken just as the waiter took a picture of the guinea pig and then carried it back to the kitchen to be dismembered.

As the carcass passed our table, I decided to forgo the diaper remark and instead reminded Abigail that I was not completely inexperienced in eating critters that looked as if they had just scurried out from under a drainpipe. I'd visited Louisiana once to look into the state's scheme to eat its way out of the nutria crisis. Nutrias were introduced into Louisiana from South America just before the Second World War, and after the trappers lost interest in them because of a dip in the price of nutria fur, they had proliferated to the point of threatening to devastate the state's vital marshland. State officials figured they might be able to encourage trapping if, in addition to the price of the fur, nutrias were valued as an exotic foodstuff. In the interests of scientific inquiry, I'd eaten nutria chili, nutria fricassee, pan-fried nutria tenderloins, and nutria sauce piquante à la fontenot.

A nutria is, not to boast, much less appetizing-looking than a guinea pig. It's about the shape and size of a small beaver—except for the tail, which is, I'm afraid, more or less the tail of a rat. There are other features that do not please. The guard hairs that cover the fur usable for coats are a snarl. The nutria's hind feet are webbed, which somehow does not make a nice contrast with its front feet. It has four clearly visible incisors, two up and two down—wide and curved and exceedingly long and, well, not to put too fine a point on it, orange. Although the two animals do have a certain familial resemblance—given that resemblance, Louisiana might find it advantageous to join forces with Peru to form a Rodent Marketing Board—it is perfectly obvious that a man who has consumed a nutria has nothing to fear from a small animal that does not even have a tail, not to speak of orange teeth.

I also reminded Abigail that trout was almost as much of a specialty of the area as guinea pig, and that I had ordered trout ceviche—a bold move into freshwater ceviche that I considered the equivalent of going to Wisconsin and ordering, say, walleye sashimi. I'd also had ceviche in Arequipa, squeezing a sea bass version in between stuffed pepper stops, and it was already clear to me that Peruvians and Ecuadorians have different notions of what authentic ceviche is. In Peru, ceviche is not something soupy that comes in a bowl; it would not ordinarily include additives like tomatoes. It is, essentially, chunks of fish (or shrimp or some combination of shellfish) and spices and shredded onions—served on a plate, eaten with a fork, and flanked by a couple of thick wedges of potato or corn. I would imagine that Peruvians consider their version of ceviche stately and Ecuadorians consider it dull.

Abigail and I had a lot of it. In the Lima shorefront neighborhood of Chorrillos, we visited a couple of spots that had a dozen or two cevicherías side by side in a single ramshackle shed. At La Costa Verde, one of the vast and somewhat overblown Lima restaurants built out into the Pacific, a waiter wearing a tuxedo served us ceviche Don Raúl, a scallop and shrimp and mushroom mixture that, according to the menu, was a contender for culinary honors at the World Exposition in Seville in 1992.

About an hour south of Lima, in Pucusana, a fishing village that is also the site of some flashy vacation houses, we came across a neatly dressed young man behind a cart of the sort hot dog vendors use in New York. He was wearing a baseball cap and an exceedingly white T-shirt. He had set up shop just a few yards from the market shed where the local fishermen brought in their catch. A couple of umbrellas shaded the cart, and a half dozen plastic stools had been placed on one side for customers. A sign announced that the young man was a specialist in instant ceviche. After a customer had ordered, the instant ceviche specialist went to work, using a stainless steel kitchen bowl as a sort of wok. He squeezed a few hyperacidic little lemons onto the fish, then added chopped-up celery and garlic and peppers and a little water and shredded onions. He stirred and cut with practiced motions—at one point flicking a bit of the sauce on the back of his hand so he could check the balance of spices with a quick taste. The entire ceviche-making process couldn't have taken more than thirty or forty seconds. After he'd placed my ceviche on a plate, he hesitated for a moment, then tossed onto the side of the plate a handful of *cancha*. Abigail seemed to catch the relief on my face. Although I hadn't mentioned it to her, *cancha* has an entry all its own on my Register of Frustration and Deprivation. In New York, it happens to be harder to come by than ceviche is.

Not that I had any complaints about the ceviche, even when it was unaccompanied by *cancha*. The one dished out by the specialist in instant ceviche was first-rate, and so was the one I had across the street, in a restaurant called Bahia-Turistica, an hour later. I was having trouble keeping my focus, though, because other dishes crowded in on the ceviches like so much tasty static. This problem was particularly acute at Costanera 700, a Lima seafood restaurant whose proprietor, Humberto Sato, is spoken of by ceviche hounds like Douglas Rodriguez in tones approaching reverence. Mr. Sato named his restaurant after its address—a service to customers, since there is no sign. Like a lot of serious seafood restaurants in Lima—or serious purveyors of Arequipeña specialties in Arequipa, for that matter—Costanera 700 is open only for the midday meal. It's in a line of buildings on the water edge of the less than uplifting Lima neighborhood of San Miguel. Its main dining room, while not unpleasant, suggests a smallish airplane hangar. Our cabdriver had a difficult time finding Costanera 700, and was not convinced we had made it even after he'd arrived. The drivers of important politicians and businessmen apparently have no such problem; they're familiar with the route.

Humberto Sato turned out to be a preternaturally calm man of Japanese ancestry who speaks about fish in the tones a master furniture maker might use to discuss fruitwoods. His menu offered five sorts of ceviche. Abigail and I ordered Ceviche Costanera, which is made with olive oil, and Ceviche La Paz, a Peruvian coastal ceviche that takes on a yellowish color from the peppers used to season it. The ceviches were perfect: the tastes of the fish and the marinade and the spices blended together with great subtlety. We figured that before we went on to the *tiradito*—a Peruvian form of ceviche in which the fish is in slices, as in sashimi, instead of in chunks and is usually served without onions—we'd vary the meal with shrimp served sizzling on an iron griddle. That dish can sometimes be no more than a garlic delivery system, but not in Sato's hands. Encouraged, we tried the *chita*, a fish I'd never heard of, cooked inside a cast of salt—which the waiter carefully cracked open, like an experienced orthopedist freeing up a mended ankle. Then we had rice with tiny shrimp. At that point, the *tiradito* was simply an impossibility. I comforted myself with the thought that we were about to go to Ecuador, where something like *tiradito* would probably be thought of as nothing more than a good start.

"**B**e careful. Save room," Douglas Rodriguez said. "We're on our way to Mecca." He kept on eating as he spoke.

Led by an Ecuadorian friend of Douglas's named Humberto Mata, we'd arrived at one of those multi-cevichería buildings in Playas, a town an hour or so west of Guayaquil. Our eventual destination was the resort town of Salinas, where Douglas had predicted we'd have the best ceviche in Ecuador at a place he'd once visited called La Lojanita. The building in Playas was a large shed that had a thatched roof and used split-bamboo fences to carve out separate outdoor dining areas for a dozen or so cevicherías with names like Cevichería Brisas del Mar and Cevichería Viagra Marina— the latter an allusion, I assumed, to the widespread belief in that part of South America that ceviche is useful not only as a hangover cure but as a sexual tonic. ("Anything with that much acid in it can't actually be good for hangovers," I had been told by a resident of Lima, who was mum on the sexual tonic issue.) The cevichería we'd chosen was a corner establishment called Fuente del Sabor, or Source of Taste, and the food made Douglas's warning difficult to heed. After some fine black-clam ceviche, we had been served *patacones* (chunks of plantain pressed down into the frying pan with a wooden mallet until about the size of a cocktail party crab cake), a spectacular seafood and rice combination, and a huge oyster that, after having been pried open with a hammer and chisel, had been covered with cheese and butter and mustard and cooked right on the flame of the range, with its enormous shell acting as the cooking vessel.

The ceviche gang was on its second day of eating. In Guayaquil, our haul had included a ceviche with so much tomato that it veered toward the fish cocktails of Veracruz and, in a simple but spectacular restaurant called Los Arbolitos, a sort of mixed stew platter that included a tripe stew, a fish stew, a mixture of salt cod and onions, and, perched on top of the pile like a jolly hat on somebody wearing a dull brown uniform, a fish ceviche. We'd eaten fish in a peanut sauce that tasted almost like curry, plus a sort of onion soup with tuna. At a place that looked as if it might serve plastic food—a place called Churrin Churron in a flashy shopping center called Mall de Sol, which also had a Pizza Hut and a Dunkin' Donuts, we'd eaten a chocolate-filled *churro* that Abigail said was worth the trip to South America.

We had also eaten *fanesca*—an astonishing fish and vegetable soup, nearly as thick as porridge, which is available in Ecuador only during Holy Week. In the Quito market, on the day after Palm Sunday, I'd noticed signs saying ¡HOY FANESCA! By Tuesday, I'd eaten it three times. As I worked on the rice and shellfish in Playas, I found myself wondering what good deed I might have done long ago that resulted in my landing in Ecuador by accident during Holy Week. In other words, I was trying to anticipate ceviche at La Lojanita while daydreaming about *fanesca* and shoveling in a shellfish and rice dish I couldn't seem to stop eating. "Save room," Douglas said again, as he carved off another piece of the oyster. "Don't forget about Mecca."

La Lojanita turned out to be a couple of blocks inland from the Salinas beach, just past a cevichería cluster called Ceviche-landia. It was an open-air place, with permanent stools lined up in front of a counter on two sides. Its sign was further proof that the Coca-Cola company had a lock on cevichería signage in Ecuador and Peru. Douglas did the ordering, and I could hear him go down the list, almost like a chant—black clam, octopus, regular shrimp, shrimp in the manner normally used for langostino (which were unavailable), sea bass with the sort of mustard sauce usually accompanying crab (also unavailable), mixed. As we settled onto the stools, I looked around and realized that much of the ceviche gang had fallen by the wayside. Douglas and his publisher, Phil Wood, and his ceviche chef, Adrian Leon, and I were the only ones left at the counter. In front of us I counted twenty bowls of ceviche.

"Do you think you really have to taste every single one?" Alice asked from the sidelines.

I did think I had to taste every single one. I couldn't let the side down. We grabbed spoons, and started. Everyone remarked on the glories of the black clam. After Adrian tasted the second type of shrimp, I heard him mutter, "Russian dressing." I was trying to keep up with the rest of the gang, even though it did occur to me that Humberto Sato and other masters of the Peruvian version of ceviche would probably describe most of what we were eating with whatever Spanish phrase translates roughly into "gussied up." Douglas praised the octopus but thought that, all in all, La Lojanita was not quite as good as it had been on his previous visit. It was possible that the proprietor had become distracted, he said, since the splendor of her ceviche had led to her being elected mayor of Salinas.

I woke up the next morning feeling a bit fragile. For some reason, I was imagining the Seville culinary competition Abigail and I had seen mentioned on La Costa Verde's menu. I envisioned it as purely a ceviche contest. The judges appeared to be Sevillano gazpacho experts pressed into service, although there were also some of those stone-faced East Germans who always seem to be among those judging Olympic diving competitions. The instant ceviche man was there, again in a baseball cap and a crisp white T-shirt, practicing his moves in the corner. Manuel Noriega paced back and forth, glowering at his competitors in an attempt to frighten them away. Rick Bayless walked in from Chicago carrying a huge marlin on a sling across his back, the way Indian women at the Otavalo market sometimes carry full-grown sheep. Off to the side, Humberto Sato, dressed in street clothes rather than his chef's whites, stood silently, having decided to withdraw because the fish were not up to his standards. Some health-food demonstrators who objected to the acid in ceviche were parading around with signs that said, "If it does that to a sea bass, think of what it's doing to you!" I wasn't planning to stay for the judging. I'd decided to take a day or two off from ceviche eating.

A couple of days later, we were back at Hacienda Cusin—the rare example of a place that has been restored into complete comfort with no accompanying glitz. I was sitting in one of the courtyards, having a chat about *fanesca* with the chef, Marco Yanez, who had provided us with a particularly splendid example on Good Friday. An explanation of its preparation makes *fanesca* sound like something that should appear on an absolutely accurate menu as Potage Labor Intensive. It has to include twelve grains and beans, to represent the twelve apostles—each ingredient soaked and cooked and dried and peeled separately. The base, salt cod cooked in milk, is thickened with peanuts; naturally, it's mandatory to start with raw peanuts, then toast them, then peel them, then grind them. I could see why *fanesca* is eaten only during Holy Week: when some frantically slurping teenager calls out, "Mom, can we have this again next week?" it stands to reason that Mom, her fingers sore from peeling corn kernels and fava beans, would answer, "Talk to me in about a year, buster."

Fanesca must be, among other things, a restorative: with a couple of bowls of it under my belt, I felt as if I had downed a couple of *Vuelve a la Vidas* or taken a few shocks from a jumper cable. I was able to begin my next lunch by enthusiastically polishing off a shrimp ceviche and a hearts of palm ceviche. Even while I was eating the ceviche, though, I found myself calculating how many more *fanesca* opportunities I'd have before Easter Sunday. I couldn't help wondering if, assuming the labor-cost issue could be sorted out, some restaurant in New York—maybe even some restaurant in lower Manhattan—might be induced to put *fanesca* on its menu. In New York, of course, there'd be no reason to be overly strict about the custom of serving it only during Holy Week. When the ingredients were available, a sign on the restaurant would announce ¡HOY FANESCA!

6.

NEW GRUB STREETS

—
—

In Chinatown, on the corner of East Broadway and Forsyth Street, a sandwich that I bought from a street vendor started me wondering whether I could consider myself a chowhound. Did I, that is, conform to the standards of the breed set forth by a Web site called chowhound.com, which describes its devotees as people who "blaze trails, combing gleefully through neighborhoods for hidden culinary treasure," people who "spurn trends and established opinion and sniff out secret deliciousness on their own"? The sandwich did possess deliciousness, and you could say that it kept at least one secret even from me: since the vendor didn't speak English, I wasn't able to figure out precisely what was in it. Chowhoundishly (on the Web site, the word can be morphed into just about any part of speech), I do regularly comb through at least one neighborhood, Chinatown—two if you count my own neighborhood, which is only a short bike ride away. I've always spent a certain amount of time in such wanderings, most of it with my mouth full. It should be said that when I began my visits to Chinatown, in the early sixties, there wasn't much to buy from a street vendor, unless your craving was for firecrackers. At that time, Chinatown was a small island below Little Italy—a small island that seemed to be getting smaller, as if it were being eroded by the constant lapping of olive oil and Chianti at its borders.

In the early sixties, there had been virtually no legal immigration from China for decades. Chinatown then had only a single, small dim sum parlor and not many other restaurants whose menus varied significantly from the sort of Americanized fare being served by descendants of Chinese railroad workers in Denver or Chinese fruit pickers in Sacramento; what was available was mostly the Chinese equivalent of the red sauce and pasta that defined Italian restaurants in the years before most New Yorkers knew that mozzarella could have any connection at all with a *bufalo*. At one of the more culinarily advanced places we frequented in Chinatown, what we considered a particularly exotic dish was, upon reflection, exotic mainly for the way it was listed on the menu: Shredded Three Kinds Meat.

This was prior to the Immigration Act of 1965, in the years when this country's immigration policy, based on a system of national quotas, reflected not simply bigotry but the sort of bigotry that seemed to equate desirable stock with blandness in cooking. The quota for the United Kingdom was so high that it was never filled. For just about any country you could visit without taking the precaution of packing your own lunch, quotas were ridiculously low. Asians were, in effect, excluded. Given the paucity of exotic newcomers, the immigrant cultures of New York were principally remnants of the great turn-of-the-century migrations from southern and eastern Europe that had ended with the quota system in the twenties. Thirty-second Street, a couple of blocks from Herald Square, hadn't begun to resemble a bustling commercial street in Seoul. Carroll Gardens did not yet offer its residents a choice of Yemeni cafés. Travelers to Coney Island expected to find Nathan's hot dogs but not Azerbaijani *kufta-boʒbash*. Although I am perfectly aware that only a person lacking in sensitivity would compare the problem of living in a place that offered a narrow range of truly interesting restaurants with the problem of involuntary servitude, I have to say that some serious eaters think of the Immigration Act of 1965 as their very own Emancipation Proclamation.

In an era when immigrants traveled by plane rather than steerage, New York, of course, was not the only place affected by the changes in immigration policy. During a trip to Southern California in the eighties, I was taken to lunch in Orange County, once a symbol of white-bread Republicanism. The restaurant was in what seemed to be a typical Southern California shopping mall—massive blocks of stores on either side of a double lane, vast parking lots—except that the entire place was Vietnamese. The signs were in Vietnamese. The salespeople were Vietnamese. The shoppers were Vietnamese. The tape store sold Vietnamese tapes, and the supermarket stocked Vietnamese vegetables. The restaurant we ate in, as I remember it, specialized in the dishes of Hue. It was as if a troupe of players had wandered onto the wrong set and had gone right on with the play they'd rehearsed anyway.

The impact on New York, though, was particularly dramatic. Once the effects of the 1965 changes began to kick in, a burgeoning Chinatown gradually swallowed great chunks of what had been Little Italy. We eventually had a profusion of not just Peking Duck but Duck Tongues and Deboned Duck Feet with Jellyfish and Chinese Flowering Chives with Shredded Duck. Eventually, I found that I could eat splendidly in Chinatown without leaving my bicycle. On Mott Street—before crossing Canal, which was once Chinatown's uptown border—I often walk my bike along a terrifically busy market block where shoppers are carefully poking exotic vegetables or reaching into a bucket of frogs to pull one out and inspect whatever it is you inspect about a frog. There, I sometimes pick up some fish balls from a woman who sells them from a large plastic bag right at the curb. Most of her customers presumably take them home and put them in soup. As I shoulder my way through the crowds, I pop them in my mouth, like jujubes.

On the other side of Canal Street, I call on a couple of places I was told about some years ago by a friend of mine named Colette Rossant, whose commitment to sniffing out secret deliciousness in Chinatown has always made Christopher Columbus's commitment to seeking a new trade route to India seem rather half hearted. Still on Mott, I visit a window to get an order of grilled daikon radish cakes that are similar to what some of the vast new dim sum restaurants serve as taro cakes. Then, on Division Street, I check the window of New South Wind Coffee Shop to make sure they haven't sold out of the specialty that's otherwise on display there, lean my bike against the window, dart in for a moment, and emerge with a rolled-up rice noodle studded with bits of some substances whose origin I do not intend to investigate.

By the time I've taken care of the rice noodle, I'm often too full to stop at Fried Dumplings on Mosco for a, well, fried dumpling, or at its rival around the corner, Tasty Dumplings, where I go for the egg-and-chive pancake. There's no longer any question of sitting down in an actual restaurant or even of stopping for dessert at the shed of the Hong Kong Egg Cake Lady, who makes some musket-ball-shaped items that I've referred to in the past as "what madeleines would taste like if the French really understood such things."

It was on the way home from one of these rambles that I stopped my bike on East Broadway and Forsyth, where street vendors were selling several unfamiliar items. What caught my eye was a sandwich, tightly wrapped in clear plastic. It consisted of an ordinary Western-style bun—what I assume the Chinese would refer to with some word that translates literally as "the sort of bread foreign devils eat"—and something green peeking out of the middle. I risked a dollar for a taste. Inside the bun was a chopped vegetable that might have been bok choy or mustard greens, flavored with something that tasted like horseradish. I loved it. Whenever I was in Chinatown during the next few weeks, I'd pick up a few greens sandwiches and hand them out when I got back to the Village, like trophies from an adventure abroad. When a recipient of my largesse gobbled up the sandwich with great enthusiasm, I beamed with pride. When someone took a couple of bites, thanked me with elaborate courtesy, and carefully folded the plastic around the remains, I made an instantaneous diagnosis: wooden palate syndrome. It turns out that you don't have to know what's in a sandwich to feel proprietary about it.

Then a thought occurred to me: This is chowhound stuff. I couldn't help thinking of the Arepa Lady. Jim Leff, who presides over chowhound.com and sometimes refers to himself as the Alpha Dog, has called the Arepa Lady "pretty much my signature 'find.'" Although Leff's site is basically a collection of message boards for the food obsessed, it has also included such features as "What Jim Had for Dinner" and "When Bad Food Happens to Good People," plus an occasional special report. The Arepa Lady of Jackson Heights, Queens, rated a special report. Late on weekend evenings, Leff wrote, she grills the Colombian corn cakes called *arepas* at Seventy-ninth and Roosevelt Avenue. This is underneath the elevated tracks used by the No. 7 subway train as it passes over the cooking odors of several dozen countries on its route from Times Square to a booming second Chinatown that has developed since 1965 in Flushing. Because of the rumble of the No. 7, you often have to shout to be heard on Roosevelt Avenue, and what you're likely to be shouting is "What a *samosa*!" or "That's the best *taco al carbón* I've had outside of Mexico!" Thanks to the Immigration Act of 1965, Roosevelt Avenue is the sort of place where someone who has just downed some Filipino barbecue may emerge from the restaurant and, in the next block or two, be tempted to follow that up with an Afghan shish kebab, a Mexican *torta*, an Indian *dosa*, and a Tibetan *momo* before making the decision about whether to go with Korean or Uruguayan baked goods. For devout chowhounds, the route of the No. 7 is El Camino de Santiago.

On this almost sacred ground, Leff cautions, you have to

search among the vendors for "the tiny, ageless woman with the beatific smile"—the Arepa Lady, serving what Leff has called his favorite food in New York. "The *arepas* themselves are snacks from heaven," his special report says. "You try one, and your first reaction is 'mmm, this is delicious.' But before that thought can fully form, waves of progressively deeper feelings begin crashing, and you are finally left silently nodding your head. You understand things. You have been loved." When the Alpha Dog finds something he likes, he eschews restraint.

Compared with the Arepa Lady, the vendor I'd just patronized did lack a certain remoteness. There wasn't any question in my mind that her very convenience made the experience less chowhoundish than it might have been. New Yorkers who revel in chowhoundry tend to do most of their eating in the outer boroughs—particularly in Queens and Brooklyn, where a lot of the people admitted in the place of all those Englishmen have congregated. Judged by the standards of people who post messages on chowhound.com, I am a stranger to the boroughs. Given the variety and quality of food available within walking distance of my house, I'm reluctant to leave Lower Manhattan at mealtime. A vendor of exotic foodstuffs is not likely to be discovered in an obscure neighborhood by someone who doesn't even like to go uptown.

My vicarious experience in outer-borough eating, on the other hand, has been quite extensive. In the early nineties, before the Internet made chowhound.com possible, I'd begun to follow the travels of a food critic named Robert Sietsema, whose dispatches I read first in an occasional newsletter he puts out called *Down the Hatch* and then in *The Village Voice*.

Although *Down the Hatch* began with a concentration on Manhattan, Sietsema was soon spending a lot of his time in places
like a Haitian nightclub on Flatbush Avenue or a Portuguese
churrasqueira off the Jericho Turnpike or an Arab diner in
Astoria or a Ghanaian seafood restaurant in the Bronx. When
he roamed around Ridgewood or Rego Park—places I'd
never been to—I thought of him as someone representing me.
At the time, I hadn't met Sietsema, but I took to calling him
"my man Sietsema." As Alice and I perused different publica-
tions over breakfast, she would occasionally comment on the
news—"Looks like they've got another truce in Northern Ire-
land," say, or "The Fed is apparently going to cut the interest
rate"—and I would say, "My man Sietsema's been eating at an
Egyptian fish joint in Brooklyn," or "My man Sietsema has
visited the best Oaxacan restaurant in New Brunswick." You
might say that I followed Sietsema's adventures to the outer
boroughs and beyond the way some sedentary Victorian
burgher in Manchester or Leeds must have followed the travels of Henry Stanley in Africa.

Eventually, my man Sietsema was not the only adventurer
I followed. A handful of professional food writers in New
York spend enough time in out-of-the-way restaurants to be
able to disagree among themselves about where to find the
best Salvadoran *pupusa* or a superior Albanian *burek*. (Both of
these turn out to be versions of meat or cheese inside of
dough; anyone who spends a lot of time trying unfamiliar
cuisines in the boroughs may come away with the impression
that most things turn out to be versions of meat or cheese
inside of dough.) Writers who concentrate on what is sometimes called ethnic eating or alternative eating or offbeat eat-

ing form a small, occasionally bickering community, like a
community of drama critics who concentrate on Off Broadway. Or maybe Off Off Broadway. Some of them hang out,
electronically, on chowhound.com, along with any number of
chat board regulars who often express their opinions with the
assuredness of food critics who simply don't happen to have
an official affiliation right at the moment.

Some of them—Myra Alperson, for instance, who pub-
lishes a newsletter called *NoshNews* ("Nosh your way from
Odessa to Bombay . . . and never leave New York")—are
virtually full-time in the neighborhoods. Others, like Eric Asimov, who writes the "$25 and Under" restaurant column for
The New York Times, make occasional forays as part of their
assignment to review inexpensive restaurants. They have produced a number of guidebooks, including Sietsema's *The Food
Lover's Guide to the Best Ethnic Eating in New York City* and
Leff's *The Eclectic Gourmet Guide to Greater New York City.*
The Los Angeles equivalent would be Jonathan Gold's
Counter Intelligence. Members of the community do not limit
themselves to the cooking of new immigrants. They're interested in food that has been here for decades—chitterlings in
Harlem, say, or blintzes in Borough Park or spleen sandwiches
in the Italian Bronx. On chowhound.com, Leff insists that a
true chowhound's lust for "hyperdeliciousness in all forms"
includes the form of foie gras and Château Margaux. Still, an
adventurous eater in New York is not likely to spend his time
in the latest chic Manhattan hot spot while there are Nigerian
yam porridge outposts in Brooklyn left to explore. Sietsema,
who has a particular interest in Africa, lists in his book New
York restaurants specializing in the food of Ethiopia, Somalia,

South Africa, Senegal, Ivory Coast, Guinea, and Mali. The index of Jonathan Gold's *Counter Intelligence* lists forty restaurants under the category of Mexican, eleven under Korean, and one under French.

Over the years, I've come to know several members of this community, and when I've talked to, say, Sietsema or to Sylvia Carter, who began writing the "Eats" column for *Newsday* in 1980 and is sometimes referred to as the den mother of the alternative eaters, or to Ed Levine, who became familiar with the boroughs when he began his food-writing career searching out places to shop, I feel positively sedentary by comparison. At some point, it occurred to me that despite the hymns I'd sung for years to the 1965 Immigration Act, I might not be completely emancipated. I couldn't claim to have availed myself of what the cover of Leff's book calls "The Undiscovered World of Hyperdelicious Offbeat Eating in All Five Boroughs." Also, I had suspected for some time that the Register of Frustration and Deprivation kept by these alternative eaters is not as extensive as the one I've maintained all these years. I had suspected, I suppose, that when they got a hankering for a dish they'd loved somewhere else in the world they could just hop on the No. 7, walk into some Queens restaurant that I've never heard of, and order an absolute clone of what they'd eaten in a Greek fishing village or a dive in Macao. They might experience almost daily the sort of adventure I triggered by mentioning ceviche to José as we drove through Queens in his Town Car. Eventually, I decided to get in touch with Leff, and when I phoned him, he asked if we should get together for a meal.

"Sure," I said.

"Great," Leff said. "You want to go to Danbury for goulash?"

That, I thought, was the Alpha Dog talking.

On chowhound.com, a battalion of food crazies stands ready to respond promptly and forthrightly if a complete stranger wants to know where to obtain the best version of a certain Vietnamese sandwich or asks if there are any modestly priced restaurants his parents might like when they come from Moline for a visit or seeks opinions on whether her friend's birthday splurge this year should be at 11 Madison Park rather than at the Gramercy Tavern or demonstrates an obvious need of being corrected by a more knowledgeable person on what to order in some new Chinese restaurant in Sunnyside. In fact, Leff assured me that if I posted news of my Chinatown sandwich, I would know within a few hours not only its precise ingredients but maybe even where to get a better one. Eric Asimov has said that chowhound.com, with its generous exchange of information by people who are similarly obsessed, is just what a Web site was meant to be, which may be another way of saying that it doesn't make money.

Although food has been a passion for Jim Leff at least since high school, when he started sending restaurant tips to Sylvia Carter at *Newsday*, he makes his living in large part as a musician—a trombonist with a leaning toward jazz and a willingness to play Hasidic dance music if that's what the gig calls for. According to Sietsema, who played in a rock band himself for a number of years while making his living at the typing and book designing and photo editing he refers to as "urban roustabout work," Leff is a "bizarrely talented" trombonist. Asimov is a guitarist, and Jonathan Gold spent years playing the amplified cello in a punk rock band. Ed Levine used to manage a jazz club in the Village. Someone might be able to put together a theory about a part of the brain that controls both offbeat food yearnings and an ear for rock or jazz music, but the way Sietsema explains it is that once you make the sound check late in the afternoon you've got nothing to do for four or five hours but search around in a strange neighborhood for someplace to get dinner.

Leff might be picked out of a crowded restaurant by someone told to look for the musician. A bearded, informally dressed man in his late thirties, he has dark hair pulled back into a knot. I've heard Leff and Sietsema and Gold and some members of what Leff calls his Fress Team—the *fressers* (Yiddish for eaters, or maybe trenchermen) who sometimes accompany him to a new restaurant he's trying—described as looking like "guys who stayed in graduate school too long." (Leff, in fact, did some graduate work, and Sietsema actually spent five years in graduate school at the University of Wisconsin, apparently without displaying any unseemly interest in a degree. Gold's *Counter Intelligence* begins, "For a while in my early twenties, my only clearly articulated ambition was to eat at least once at every restaurant on Pico Boulevard, starting with the fried *yuca* dish served at a *pupusería* near where the street began in downtown Los Angeles and working methodically westward toward the chili fries at Tom's #5 near the beach. It seemed a reasonable enough alternative to graduate school at the time.") If they showed up anonymously to review a fancy French restaurant on the Upper East Side, the question might be not whether the headwaiter would recognize them but whether he would be willing to seat them. The answer is presumably yes: Gold, who might be considered the alternative eaters' first crossover act, eventually made his way from Pico Boulevard to reviewing mainstream New York restaurants for *Gourmet*.

My first glimpse of Leff did not turn out to be in a goulash restaurant in Danbury. Danbury seemed a long way to go for goulash, although Leff assured me that it was only an hour away, that the journey would include a stop at a homemade yoghurt place in Elmhurst which also does great spinach pie, and that eating the Danbury goulash would almost certainly be an experience that made a significant impact on my life. He was also quick to say that the goulash place had not been discovered by him but by Jane and Michael Stern, who have been sniffing out unpretentious restaurants around the country for a number of years—although he was willing to take credit for discovering, in a manner of speaking, that the Sterns had underrated it.

Leff's eagerness to take me to what was, in effect, someone else's restaurant seemed to refute what other alternative eaters had told me about his singular attachment to restaurants that he has himself discovered. Most food writers who report on the offbeat pay at least lip service to the notion that it's of no real importance who happened to write about a restaurant first. Leff seems unembarrassed about using "Major Discovery" as a headline or referring to a restaurant as "my greatest discovery ever." He is exquisitely conscious of which restaurants were mentioned first on chowhound.com, reflecting the territorial instincts you might expect to encounter in an alpha dog. Jonathan Gold—who, like Robert Sietsema, has at times felt unwelcome on chowhound.com—has called Leff "the premier proponent of the paranoid school of restaurant criticism."

On the other hand, I can understand taking some pride in a signature find. Witness how I feel about my greens sandwich. Discovery is part of the game. Also, discovery is hard work. Sietsema wears out a copy of Hagstrom's *New York City 5 Borough Atlas* every year as he prowls the streets, becoming particularly alert when he goes through a neighborhood in which, as he has put it, "the hipster coefficient is zero." When Sietsema reads in a neighborhood newspaper about a homicide in some bar described as a place frequented by West Africans, he finds himself wondering not about the victim or the crime but about whether the bar happens to be the sort of bar that serves food.

Sietsema has said that once a writer discovers a place he may feel the necessity to "defend it against all comers." If others are unimpressed with it, after all, it wasn't much of a discovery. When I accompanied Ed Levine one day for a lunchtime outing in Queens—we'd started on Roosevelt Avenue with a Cuban sandwich at El Sitio and some *picaditas con carne* at a *taquería* called El Grano de Oro 2000, then finished up in Corona with an *empanada* at El Palacio de Empanada and a sublime eggplant parmigiana sandwich at the Corona Heights Pork Store, those two treats separated by what you might call a palate cleanser of old-fashioned Italian lemon ice in a paper cup at Benfaremo, the Lemon Ice King of Corona—he did his impression of Jim Leff's response to hearing another eater's disappointment in, say, a Salvadoran *pupusería* Leff had discovered: "But the chef went back to El Salvador. You didn't *know?* The mama's only in the kitchen on Thursday. You went on a Tuesday? You didn't *know?*"

The moment a restaurant is discovered, of course, it stands exposed to the danger of going downhill. It might indeed lose its cook to the constant back-and-forth of modern immigration. It might become self-conscious from having attracted what Leff refers to with great contempt as "Zagat-clutching foodies"—a foodie being in his lexicon precisely what a chowhound is not. For a while, chowhound.com actually had a department called "Downhill Alert." I once heard Leff say that the entire route of the No. 7 was going downhill. This was not long after the route, which has often been mentioned in the mainstream press, became the subject of a piece by Jonathan Gold in *Gourmet,* foodie central. (In the piece, Gold, perhaps innocently, mentioned that he'd never been able to find the Arepa Lady.) "The Indians are gone, and it's mostly Pakistanis," Leff said of the No. 7. "And I love Pakistani food, but these particular Pakistanis have sort of agreed not to cook it well, so there's not really good Indian food anymore. The Colombians . . . that are left are sort of hapless, and are not cooking that great. The Mexicans coming in—we had great hopes—but there's a lot of bad Mexican food now in Jackson Heights."

The thrill of discovery is obviously enhanced by discovering something rare, or even unique. One of my forays with Leff included a lunch (if that's what the second or third meal you eat in the middle of the day is called) at a kosher Middle

Eastern restaurant in Brooklyn called Olympic Pita, a place
that I at first thought I'd been brought to because of a design
element new to my experience: a large picture window in the
dining room faced straight into the back of a one-car garage, a
few feet away. The back of the garage had been totally covered in a forest (or maybe jungle) mural that blended with
some bushes in the narrow grassy strip in front of it and with
the green of the asphalt shingles on the roof. Leff then told
me that what I would find truly rare about Olympic Pita was
an Iraqi Jewish mango hot sauce called *amba*, which any stu-
dent of that cuisine would be astounded to find in North
America. "If you ever meet an Iraqi Jew and tell them you
know where to get this, they will doubt your word," he
informed me. "It's not considered available. It's extremely
rare. This might be the rarest single food in town." I liked
amba, which we spread generously on our *shawarma*. I
thought of having something to put over on an Iraqi Jew as a
little bonus.

All of the offbeat eaters are, of course, aware that what
seems breathtakingly exotic and authentic and even quaint
could be a trap—that they could be so smitten by the palpably
unspoiled granny bustling around the tiny kitchen in her
babushka that they overlook the rocklike quality of her
dumplings. If pressed, they will sadly report one another's
propensity for falling into the trap. Leff sometimes says that if
a place selling astonishing blueberry muffins were next door
to a so-so Mozambican place, Robert Sietsema would write
about the Mozambican place and followers of the Alpha Dog
would hear about the blueberry muffins, the chowhoundian

way being never to "ingest anything undelicious," whether it's exotic or not.

Sietsema, who believes he adheres to the nothing-undelicious principle of chowhoundishness himself, acknowledges that he takes an almost anthropological approach, even though anthropology was not one of the subjects he got around to studying during his academic career. He once told me, for instance, that he has spent some time attempting to find out why all the Uzbekistani restaurants he's tried seem to have a dish called Korean Carrots. The subject came up while we were having the second leg of lunch one day at an Uzbekistani restaurant in Forest Hills called Salut. We had started in Ridgewood, at a stand called Bosnia Express Corp., with a hamburger sandwich (a *pljeskavica*, actually) on a bun so gigantic that it made a *pan bagnat* bun look like one of those White Castle miniatures—we ate our *pljeskavicas* while sitting on an automobile seat that had been propped against the wall across from two folding chairs to create the sort of sidewalk café one might expect to find in an area of the Balkans that had seen its share of trouble—and we would finish off with a *masala dosa* in a tiny café called Dosa Hutt, next to an ornate Hindu temple in Flushing. One theory he has come across about Korean Carrots, Sietsema said, is that one of the conditions the Japanese imposed upon Russia after winning the Russo-Japanese War was that Russia accept some of Japan's unassimilated Koreans, who were then sent to Uzbekistan. On the other hand, Sietsema, who has a penchant for irony that is rare among the food-obsessed, finds it difficult to part with the notion that the name comes from the fact that Uzbeks, like everyone else in

New York, buy carrots from fruit and vegetable stands run by Koreans. I should say that the Korean Carrots were not so-so. They were quite good. Not as good as a sort of vegetable noodle soup called *lagman,* which we'd eaten just before the carrots arrived—the *lagman* was what Leff would have called hyper-delicious—but still quite good.

Not long after I'd accompanied Leff and his Fress Team one Tuesday night to a place near Sheepshead Bay that he'd heard was "the end-all and be-all of Georgian food"—it won out as our destination over the restaurant in a Russian *schvitz* called Wall Street Bath & Day Spa—Robert Sietsema, who happens to live only a few blocks from me in the Village, came by with some early issues of *Down the Hatch* that I'd asked to see. The Fress Team outing had started me thinking about how strenuous chowhounding is—strenuous, I mean, beyond just the strain of eating two or three lunches and the tension of maintaining a constant lookout for the bagel proprietor who just might have the magic pumpernickel bagel. On the way to Sheepshead Bay, Leff had outlined some of the problems we might face. For one thing, given the language difficulties he'd encountered when he phoned the restaurant, it could turn out to be closed on Tuesdays. In case we found ourselves in need of a fallback, he'd brought along a thick printout that listed, in tiny type, all of the restaurants in his repertoire, arranged by neighborhood. Some of the restaurants were listed by name only, and some not even by name ("Irish place in back of Ping's"). Some of them included comments or favorite dishes. On the upper-left-hand corner of the first page was typed

3281, the number of restaurants on the list. Leafing through
the printout, I told Leff that it looked like the life list of a particularly maniacal birder.

He ticked off some other potential problems: maybe Tuesday was such a slow night they'd have nothing available
beyond chicken and *pelmeni*, which he has referred to as "the
ubiquitous Russian tortellini." Or maybe the menus would be
in Cyrillic characters only, meaning the glossary he'd taken
the trouble to assemble that afternoon, partly from research
on the Internet, would do him no good at all.

In chowhounding, the language problem is ever present.
So is the danger of being ensnared in the quaint-granny trap.
So is the difficulty of familiarizing yourself with dozens of
different cuisines. When we finally did get to the Georgian
restaurant and managed to order, Leff, who says that he has
eaten in every decent Georgian restaurant in New York, was
confident that the *khachapuri* (as it happens, a version of
cheese inside of dough) was insufficiently flaky, given its star-
tling resemblance to quesadillas; as someone who has traveled
extensively as a musician, he is in a position to compare, say,
salgadinhos he tries in Astoria with *salgadinhos* he has had in
Brazil. But, given the rate and variety of immigration, there
is a limit to everyone's experience. At Olympic Pita, had we
been eating a superior *amba* or only a run-of-the-mill *amba*? Is
it possible that if I did ever meet an Iraqi Jew and proudly
escorted him to Olympic Pita for a little surprise, he would
say, after a quick taste, "They told you that was *amba*?"

At my house, Sietsema and I talked a bit about the restaurants we liked in the Village. I reminded him how fortunate we
were to live in an area that offered such remarkable food only

a stroll away. I'd told him about a restaurant in Hoboken, and I realized that I liked the thought of my man Sietsema, armed with a street atlas of Hudson County, trying it out, maybe on one of those mild fall evenings when my own explorations went no farther than a stroll to a pizza parlor on Spring Street greatly treasured for its clam pie. Maybe he'd happen across a fabulous purveyor of Guyanese *rotis* or Dominican fritters on the way. Thinking about a walk downtown reminded me of my greens sandwich. I had posted it on chowhound.com, but nobody seemed interested in enlightening me about its origin or telling me where I could get a better one. I happened to have a greens sandwich in the fridge, and I offered it to Sietsema. I like to think that I hadn't prepared myself to respond to an unenthusiastic reception by saying that refrigeration is known to deaden the taste of Chinese greens or that I'd heard rumors that the regular sandwich maker had recently been picked up by Immigration.

Sietsema loved it. "It's a real find," he said. "A totally unique entity."

"Did you say 'totally unique entity'?" I said.

He had.

"Well, thank you," I said. "Thank you very much."

7.

MISSING LINKS

—
—

The news that boudin is the Cajun foodstuff I most yearn for when I'm away from Louisiana may come as a revelation to anyone who has been with me when I'm slurping gumbo in one of the anointed parishes or to those I've joined at a long picnic table that has been covered with the previous day's Lafayette *Daily Advertiser* in preparation for a crawfish boil—an event at which I'm usually remembered as the overfocused fellow at the end of the table who's clawing desperately at the shells in an effort to keep up with the more experienced peelers. It may also surprise anyone who has been nearby when I'm having a go at crawfish étouffée. Still, the fact remains that if I happened to be in Louisiana when the warden walked into my cell to discuss my last meal—I assume that by then many layers of appeals courts would have rejected the argument that the dispatching of someone who stood between me and a

table full of Cajun delicacies was justifiable as a crime of passion—boudin would be my priority. If I weren't in Louisiana,
asking for it wouldn't do any good.

When people in Breaux Bridge or Opelousas or Jeanerette
talk about boudin (pronounced "boo-DAN"), they mean a
soft mixture of rice and pork and liver and seasoning that is
squeezed hot into the mouth from a sausage casing, usually in
the parking lot of a grocery store and preferably while leaning against a pickup. (*Boudin* means "blood sausage" to the
French, most of whom would probably line up for immigration visas if they ever tasted the Cajun version.) I figure that
about eighty percent of the boudin purchased in Louisiana is
consumed before the purchaser has left the parking lot, and
most of the rest of it is polished off in the car. In other words,
Cajun boudin not only doesn't get outside the state, it usually
doesn't even get home.

When I am daydreaming of boudin, it sometimes occurs to
me that of all the indignities the Acadians of Louisiana have
had visited upon them—being booted out of Nova Scotia
before they had a chance to taste Lunenburg sausage, being
ridiculed as rubes and swamp rats by neighboring Anglo-
phones in Louisiana for a couple of centuries, being punished
for speaking their own language in the school yard—nothing
has been as deeply insulting as what restaurants outside South
Louisiana present as Cajun food.

As recently as the late seventies, it was rare even in New
Orleans, a couple of hours east of the Cajun parishes, to find
anything on a menu labeled Cajun. Around that time, Paul
Prudhomme, a Cajun from Opelousas, was working as a chef
in a renowned New Orleans restaurant called Commander's

Palace, which has no connection at all with Cajun food. Prud-homme decided that the method of cooking what was some-times called an Indian steak—tossing a steak on a ferociously hot piece of cast iron that chefs call a flat top, so that the meat was seared on the outside and juicy inside—could work with a firm-fleshed fish. He happened to try it with redfish, which is what people in Louisiana call red drum—a fish then popular mainly among sportsmen. The menu at Commander's Palace— and at Mr. B's Bistro, where Prudhomme went next—called it grilled redfish. When he became the chef of his own restau-rant in the French Quarter—K-Paul's Louisiana Kitchen, which was the first widely celebrated Cajun restaurant in New Orleans—he used a white-hot skillet instead of a flat top and called the dish blackened redfish.

It was an instant hit—so popular that he had to ration it to one order per table. Within six weeks of its introduction, he once told me, a customer reported having spotted blackened redfish on a menu in Florida. Partly through the impact of Chef Paul, a massive and magnetic figure, restaurants around the country began including on their menus what they called Cajun dishes—described sadly by Prudhomme as "burnt fish with a whole lot of pepper on it." It made no difference that the only Cajuns who had ever eaten blackened redfish were those who had traveled to New Orleans and dined at Com-mander's Palace or Mr. B's Bistro or K-Paul's Louisiana Kitchen. Although Prudhomme himself switched to black-ened tuna early on, the national redfish craze continued. In 1988 the new threat to the species forced Louisiana to ban the commercial catching of redfish in its waters. After an ambi-tious undercover operation in July 1993, wildlife agents arrested forty-five people on charges of sneaking Louisiana redfish to Mississippi and then bringing it back to sell in Louisiana—in other words, redfish laundering. Cajun came to mean "spicy," in fish fillets or potato chips, but what Cajuns actually eat continued to be pretty much ignored outside the state. For Americans who hadn't been to South Louisiana, boudin remained as foreign as *gado-gado* or *cheb*.

The scarcity of boudin in the rest of the country makes it all the more pleasurable to have a Louisiana friend who likes to travel and occasionally carries along an ice chest full of local ingredients, just in case. I happen to have such a friend in James Edmunds, of New Iberia, Louisiana. James's visits to New York have regularly included the ritualistic unpacking of an ice chest on my kitchen table. Occasionally, the ice chest has been hauled along because of a special occasion: for a party we held once in New York to celebrate American delicacies, for instance, James and his wife, Susan Hester, showed up with many pounds of boudin, and, as a prize for the guests who had come the farthest, I presented them with a volume called *The Woman's Day Book of Gelatin Cookery*. As I handed the book to James, he said, "Darn! We already have it."

But it has also been his custom to bring the ice chest simply because he has made plans to cook a meal during the visit—crawfish étouffée, for instance, or gumbo or his signature shrimp stew. James turns out gumbo that shows clear evidence of having been made by someone willing to stir the roux pot for an hour and a half, until it is minutes or maybe seconds away from being ruined by burning—an approach that the late John Foster Dulles referred to, in another context, as brinkmanship. On those trips, the ice chest would also hold some boudin. I was so eager to get my hands on the boudin that I often ate it right in the kitchen, as soon as we heated it through, rather than trying to make the experience more authentic by searching for something appropriate to lean against. In lower Manhattan, after all, it could take a while to find a pickup.

Then there came the day when I was sentenced to what I think of as medium-security cholesterol prison. (Once the cholesterol penal system was concessioned out to the manufacturers of statin drugs, medium-security cholesterol prison came to mean that the inmate could eat the occasional bit of bacon from the plate of a generous luncheon companion but could not order his own BLT.) James stopped bringing boudin, the warders having summarily dismissed my argument that the kind I particularly like—Cajun boudin varies greatly from maker to maker—was mostly just rice anyway.

I did not despair. James is inventive, and he's flexible. Once, he decided that an architect friend of his who lives just outside New Iberia made the best crawfish étouffée in the area. Like one of those research and development hotshots who are always interested in ways of improving the product, James took the trouble to look into the recipe, which had been handed down to the architect by forebears of unadulterated Cajunness. James was prepared for the possibility that one of the secret ingredients of the architect's blissful étouffée was, say, some herb available only at certain times of year in the swamps of the Atchafalaya Basin Spillway. As it turned out, one of the secret ingredients was Campbell's cream of mushroom soup. (Although crawfish étouffée, which means smothered crawfish, is one of the best-known Cajun dishes, it emerged only in the fifties, when a lot of people assumed that just about any recipe was enhanced by a can of Campbell's cream of mushroom soup.) During ensuing étouffée preparations in New York, there would come a moment when James said, in his soft South Louisiana accent, "I think this might be a good time for certain sensitive people to leave the kitchen for just a little while." Then we'd hear the whine of the can opener, followed by an unmistakable *glub-glub-glub*.

A few years after my sentence was imposed, James and I were talking on the telephone about an imminent New York visit that was to include the preparation of one of his dinner specialties, and he told me not to worry about the problem of items rattling around in his ice chest. I told him that I actually hadn't given that problem much thought, what with global warming and nuclear proliferation and all. As if he hadn't heard me, he went on to say that he'd stopped the rattling with what he called packing boudin.

"Packing boudin?"

"That's right," James said.

I thought about that for a moment or two. "Well, it's got Bubble Wrap beat," I finally said. "And we wouldn't have to worry about adding to this country's solid waste disposal problem. Except for the casing." The habit of tossing aside the casing of a spent link of boudin is so ingrained in some parts of Louisiana that there is a bumper sticker reading CAUTION— DRIVER EATING BOUDIN—a way of warning the cars that follow about the possibility of their windshields being splattered with what appear to be odd-looking insects. From that visit on, I took charge of disposing of the packing boudin whenever James was carrying his ice chest, and I tried not to dwell on my disappointment when he wasn't.

Once, I got a call from James before a business trip to New York which was not scheduled to include the preparation of a Louisiana meal—that is, a trip that would ordinarily not include boudin. He asked if he could store a turducken in my freezer for a couple of days; he was making a delivery for a friend. I hesitated. I was trying to remember precisely what a turducken is, other than something Cajuns make that seems to go against the laws of nature.

James, perhaps thinking that my hesitancy reflected some reluctance to take on the storage job, said, "There'd be rental boudin involved, of course."

"Fair's fair," I said.

W hat led to my being in Louisiana a couple of weeks later for something that James insisted on calling a boudin blitzkrieg is rather complicated. As a matter of convenience, James had picked up the rental boudin at the same place he'd bought the turducken, Hebert's Specialty Meats in Maurice, Louisiana. Hebert's is a leading purveyor of turducken, which it makes by taking the bones out of a chicken and a duck and a turkey, stuffing the chicken with stuffing, stuffing the stuffed chicken into a similarly stuffed duck, and stuffing all that, along with a third kind of stuffing, into the turkey. The result cannot be criticized for lacking complexity, and it presents a challenge to the holiday carver almost precisely as daunting as meat loaf.

The emergence of turducken in the early nineties did not

surprise Cajuns. When it comes to eating, they take improvi-
sation for granted. Some people in New Iberia, for instance,
collect the sludge left over from mashing peppers at the McIl-
henny Tabasco plant and use it to spice up the huge pots of
water they employ to boil crawfish. When Thanksgiving
approaches, they fill the same huge pots with five or six gallons of lard instead of water and produce deep-fried turkey—
a dish that is related to the traditional roast turkey in the way
that *soupe au pistou* in Provence or *ribollita* in Tuscany is
related to the vegetable soup that was served in your high
school cafeteria. Susan Hester, who works at the Iberia Parish
library, once heard a deputy sheriff who was lecturing on per-
sonal defense recommend buying water-based rather than oil-
based pepper spray not only because it comes off the clothing
easier but also because it is preferable for flavoring the meat
being grilled at a cookout.

Although I didn't want to appear ungrateful for the rental
boudin, I reminded James that by buying boudin in Maurice,
which is twenty miles from New Iberia, he was flouting the
rule promulgated by his old friend Barry Jean Ancelet, a folklorist and French professor at the University of Louisiana at
Lafayette: In the Cajun country, the best boudin is always the
boudin closest to where you live, and the best place to eat
boiled crawfish is always extraordinarily inconvenient to your
house. James is aware that this theory has a problem with
internal consistency—it means, for instance, that for him the
best boudin is at Bonin's meat market in New Iberia, and for
Barry Jean Ancelet it's at The Best Stop Super Market in
Scott—but he reconciles that by saying that Barry, being a

folklorist, has a different notion of objective truth than some other people.

We had never talked much about the source of the boudin James brought to New York, except that I knew it had changed once, some years ago, when a purveyor named Dud Breaux retired. Once James's purchase of boudin in Maurice raised the subject, though, he assured me that under ordinary circumstances he follows the Ancelet Dictum: Before leaving for New York, he stocks up at Bonin's, assuming that the proprietor happens to be in what James called "a period of nonretirement." The proprietor's name is Waldo Bonin, but he is known in New Iberia as Nook. He is a magisterial man with white hair and a white mustache and a white T-shirt and a white apron. Nook Bonin has not retired as many times as Frank Sinatra did, but he is about even with Michael Jordan.

Like one of those boxers who bid farewell to the ring with some regularity, Bonin comes back every time with a little less in his repertoire. For forty-five years or so, he and his wife, Delores, ran a full-service meat market that also included a lot of Cajun specialties. The first time they came out of retirement, they had dropped everything but boudin and cracklins (crunchy pieces of fatback that are produced by rendering lard from a hog) and hogshead cheese, plus soft drinks for those who weren't going to get back to their cars with their purchases intact. The second time, when the Bonins started reappearing only on Friday afternoons and Saturday mornings, they had dropped the cracklins. As a matter of policy, James doesn't actually eat cracklins—"I just think it's good to know that there's a line out there you're not going to cross," he has said—but as someone who depends on Nook Bonin's boudin, he had to be disturbed by what appeared to be a trend. "I wouldn't mind losing the Cokes," he has said, when envisioning what might be dropped in the Bonins' next comeback. "But it is getting kind of scary."

The recipe for the boudin sold at Bonin's is a secret. In fact, it has occurred to James that the proprietor himself may not know the secret: People customarily speak of Nook Bonin's boudin, but it is actually made by Delores Bonin, who goes heavy on the rice and uses an array of spices that, I would be prepared to testify under oath, owe nothing to the test kitchens of the Campbell's soup company. Although the Bonins have two daughters, neither of them chose to go into the family business. Anna is an administrator in a special-education program, and Melissa is an artist. James and Susan happen to be longtime admirers of Melissa's work—some years ago, they bought the first painting she ever sold—but James can't help thinking that if she had chosen to put her creative energy into boudin making rather than art, the community would not now be beset by the tension brought on by her parents' stair-step retirements. James and Susan have pinned their hopes on the Bonins' only grandchild—Melissa's son, Emile. Unfortunately, at the time the boudin blitz got us focusing on the line of succession, Emile was only ten years old. James was cheered, though, when we walked into the Bonins' store on a Saturday morning and Delores Bonin reached over the meat case to hand us a photograph of Emile posing behind the device that stuffs boudin into sausage casing. Emile was smiling.

Even assuming that Emile decides to cast his lot with

boudin, though, it will be a number of years before he's old enough to take over the business. James and I discussed that situation in the sort of conversation I can imagine a working team from State and Defense having about whether sufficient steps have been taken to guarantee that this country maintains a secure and unbroken supply of cobalt in the face of any contingency. We decided that, just in case the Bonin family line of succession does get broken, I should sample some of the possibilities for what I suppose you'd have to call replacement boudin. This is why Susan, who was carrying a cutting board and a kitchen knife, and James and I were driving around on a sunny weekend, tasting what Nook Bonin had to offer and testing out, in a judicious way, the work of other purveyors. At least that's what I would tell the penal authorities if the question ever came up.

By Sunday night, we had tried the boudin from, among other places, Legnon's Boucherie, in New Iberia, and Bruce's U-Need-A-Butcher, in Lafayette, and Poche's Meat Market and Restaurant, in Poche Bridge, and Heleaux's Grocery, also in Lafayette, and, of course, The Best Stop, in Scott. We hadn't by any measure exhausted the supply of even highly recommended boudin purveyors. For instance, we hadn't tried Johnson's Grocery, in Eunice, or Billeaud's in Broussard, a town near Lafayette that used to have an annual boudin festival. (Billeaud's is a sort of convenience store that includes gasoline among its services, and, according to what James had heard, anyone who got a fill-up of eight gallons or more also got a free link of boudin.) A friend of mine in New Orleans,

Randy Fertel, after tracking down the source of the boudin that he looks forward to eating every year at the New Orleans Jazz Fest, had recommended Abe's Cajun Market in Lake Charles, which is practically in Texas, but there hadn't been time. Still, I had tasted enough contenders for replacement boudin to tell James that I hoped Nook and Delores Bonin truly understood that for people who have been active all their lives retirement can be a trap.

I had to admit to Barry Jean Ancelet, who joined us at The Best Stop, that his local purveyor makes a distinguished link of boudin—moderate, shading toward meaty, when it comes to the all-important rice-meat ratio. A lot of people agree with Barry about The Best Stop's boudin; Lawrence Menard, who opened the place in 1986, told us that he now sells between sixty-five hundred and seven thousand pounds of boudin a week. Barry does know a lot about Cajun eating habits, and, like a lot of Cajun men, he's a serious cook. The last time I'd encountered him was when I was in Louisiana looking into the nutria-eating scheme, which was, essentially, an attempt to do to the nutria on purpose what Paul Prudhomme had done to the redfish by accident. Barry, assisted by his wife, Caroline, had prepared nutria sauce piquante to give me some idea what gourmets had to look forward to if the rodent marketing board ever got into high gear. As he stirred the pot, Barry had said that the nutria would probably have joined other swamp critters in the Cajun diet without any encouragement from the state if it had been around when poverty and isolation en-hanced Cajun inventiveness in the kitchen. By the time nutrias began to appear in the marshlands in any numbers, he said, the Second World War had already drawn a lot of Cajuns into the

cities and their first salaried jobs. As adventurous as Cajuns
are in their eating habits, the days when they were assumed
to eat just about anything are gone. As someone I met in
New Iberia had said, "Why eat nutria when you can get frozen
chicken breasts cheap at Sam's?"

At that meal, one of the Ancelets' sons, François, had put a
nutria skull on the table as a sort of centerpiece. Barry showed
me the recipe for nutria sauce piquante. It had some familiar
instructions of Cajun cooking, like "make small roux, add
onions, bell peppers, celery, and garlic" and "add parsley and
onion tops just before serving." Halfway through the meal, I
told Barry that the nutria sauce piquante was a triumph,
although I had to allow for the possibility that prepared in his
sauce piquante the Sunday *Boston Globe* would have been a triumph. Putting both the tail and the orange teeth from my
mind, I asked for seconds.

"I actually call it Nutria Caroline," Barry said, with a hint
of a bow toward his wife. "I thought of calling it Nutria
Cagney."

"Nutria Cagney?"

Barry, standing with his elbows close to his body and his
hands pointed straight ahead, said, in a Cagneyesque growl,
"You dirty rat."

In a conversation on boudin that began, appropriately, at
The Best Stop and continued later that evening in a restaurant
called Bubba Frey's, Barry explained the Ancelet Dictum to us
in more detail. A link of boudin, he said, is a clean food,
essentially treated by Cajuns as "an enclosed lunch"; it's even
cleaner if you eat the casing, which Lawrence Menard himself
always does. Boiled crawfish, on the other hand, is notoriously

messy, leaving a table piled with shells and crawfish heads. It stands to reason that you'd want to leave that kind of mess far from your lair. He pointed out that for boiled crawfish he and James both favor a place called Hawk's, whose location is inconvenient to both of them and to practically everybody else. In a book called *Cajun Country Guide,* Macon Fry and Julie Posner don't mention remoteness as Hawk's secret; they say that the reason Hawk's is so good is that Hawk Arceneaux puts his crawfish through a twenty-four-hour freshwater purging process. But, then again, they're not folklorists.

Does the reasoning behind the Ancelet Dictum mean that it's all in the mind—that people just *think* the best boudin is the one convenient to where they live? Not exactly. To illustrate that there is an objective best, Barry told us that people who attend a Saturday-morning Cajun jam session near Eunice, a town in an area known as the Cajun Prairies, tend to bring boudin for refreshments, and the locals used to sneer at boudin that wasn't from Johnson's. Then, as more and more people got a taste of what Lawrence Menard was producing, the locals started asking people driving by Scott to bring them boudin from The Best Stop. But doesn't that story destroy the basic theory? Not exactly, James said, because it's a story *told* by someone who lives five minutes from The Best Stop Super Market.

Since the *e* in Frey is silent, Bubba Frey's sounds at first like a succinct description of Southern cooking rather than a restaurant. It turned out to be a restaurant, though—a bright, knotty-pine place with a Cajun combo that included on the night we were there Bubba Frey himself as one of its fiddlers. We went there after a performance of *Rendez-vous des Cadi-*

ens, a Cajun radio show that Barry emcees every Saturday at the Liberty Theater in Eunice. For some time, Bubba Frey had run a general store in a nearby hamlet called Mowata—a name I would hope is connected with a flood or the discovery of a particularly capacious well—and at some point he decided to add a restaurant next door. Boudin balls were listed as an appetizer. Boudin isn't commonly served by restaurants, although Cafe des Amis, in Breaux Bridge, offers something called Oreille de Cochon—beignet dough that is baked in the shape of pig's ears, covered with powdered sugar, and, for an extra dollar, stuffed with boudin. It's a dollar well spent.

Boudin balls are made by rolling boudin into balls, coating them with something like Zatarain's Fish-Fry, and frying away. At Bubba Frey's, they were delicious, and the proprietor, who came over to our table between sets, told us that the boudin was made at his store next door. I told James that the next time he happened to be on the Cajun Prairies he might consider finding out what Bubba's boudin tasted like unfried. Then it occurred to me that if James liked it better than he liked Nook Bonin's boudin, he might feel obligated to move to Mowata, so as not to flout the Ancelet Dictum. James did not seem enthusiastic about that prospect. He and Susan have both lived in New Iberia all of their lives, and have a lot of friends there. Also, James subscribes to the theory that, perhaps because the French settlement of the Cajun Prairies included a strong admixture of Germans, people there are a bit stiffer than the people who live in the Cajun Bayous.

Once, in the late seventies, I celebrated Mardi Gras in Mamou, a Cajun Prairie town not far from Eunice. In the version of Mardi Gras celebrated in Mamou and the rural areas of

Evangeline Parish, it is customary for horsemen to stop at farmhouses and beg a chicken for their gumbo, which is later consumed at American Legion Evangeline Post No. 123. If the farmer tells the horsemen to help themselves, they are entitled to jump off their horses and scamper—to the extent that anyone with a quart or two of beer in him can be said to scamper—across a muddy barnyard in pursuit of a frightened hen that is more agile than it looks and has the advantage of complete sobriety. When James mentioned the supposed effect of the Germans, I tried to recall just how loose people seemed, but my memories of the occasion are dominated by the Mardi Gras riders' lunch stop, which featured boudin. I'm still not quite certain how stiffness in Cajuns would manifest itself. Maybe they use only two kinds of stuffing in their turduckens.

A couple of weeks later, I heard from James: The boudin at Bubba Frey's store was, as we suspected, excellent—"a commendable second place to Nook," James wrote, "but still not with the transcendent special taste." Moving to Mowata was not on the table. Also, he and Susan and the Bonins' daughter Melissa had gone to dinner together and, as it happened, had fallen into a little chat about the future. "I told her that if Emile learned the recipe and learned how to make boudin, he'd never starve," James said. "And neither, it goes without saying, would we."

8.

CHINATOWN, CHINATOWN

===

If I'm so intent on eating the local specialty wherever I happen to be, how, exactly, did I find myself in the market for a Chinese restaurant in Paris? The answer is complicated, but I'm pretty sure that its origins are buried somewhere in a visit I made in the late sixties to the Republic of Nauru, a tiny island nation in the Central Pacific that happens to be made mostly of high-grade phosphate. Nauru's composition means that it is more valuable as a commodity than it is as a piece of real estate, and I was there to observe the phenomenon of Nauruans becoming prosperous as the homeland they held dear was gradually carted away in the holds of large freighters. In those days, the only way to get to Nauru was on a plane that arrived from Fiji every two weeks, so even the briefest visit, such as mine, lasted what some of the Australian engineers employed by the mining operation called the statutory fortnight. Culinary opportunities seemed limited. Partly because the island is almost completely surrounded by a dangerous shelf reef rather than the barrier reef familiar from Pacific Islands travel brochures, there was no fishing fleet. Practically none of the land was arable. The areas that had been mined out were left as gnarled coral pinnacles that first-time viewers had a tendency to compare to the other side of the moon.

There were Chinese on the island as contract workers in the mining operation, though, and they had managed to grow some vegetables. Somehow, they came up with fish. They even operated a restaurant, which was called Star Twinkles. A former official of the British colonial service who worked for the Nauruan government pointed to the existence of the garden and the restaurant as confirmation of his theory, developed over years of service in the Pacific, that the Overseas Chinese are a superior race. Being resistant to racial theories, even those that assign only positive attributes to the race being discussed, I pointed out that, just for starters, some scientists might question whether Overseas Chinese can be said to be a race, distinct from, say, Chinese who remained in China. But every time I was about to dismiss the theory as unscientific and perhaps even repugnant I'd have a meal at Star Twinkles. Despite what seemed to be insurmountable obstacles to obtaining appropriate ingredients, Star Twinkles was a magnificent restaurant. Since then, in places as unlikely as port cities in South America or farm towns in western Kansas, I suppose I harbor the belief that just around the corner, unlikely as it seems, there could be another Star Twinkles. In my memory, after all of these years, Star Twinkles still, well, shines.

Take Little Rock. During Bill Clinton's administration, it turned out that one of the people caught up in a scandal over White House fund-raising had run a Chinese restaurant in

Little Rock while the Great Scarfer was governor. It wouldn't have surprised me to learn that the restaurant, which was popular with the political crowd, served food at the Star Twinkles level. Sure, the proprietor may have adapted his menu a bit to make legislators from places like Mount Ida and Ash Flat feel comfortable in an Oriental setting. I could imagine menu items like Bubba's Delight or Hush Puppies Szechuan Style or General Tyson's Chicken. Still, given my experience in Nauru, I saw no reason why it couldn't be an excellent Chinese restaurant, even if it had a locally appropriate name like The Jade Goober.

Once, through a mix-up of scheduling, Alice and I found ourselves in Cuenca, a lovely old city in Ecuador, on the day before Shrove Tuesday—a day, as it turns out, when virtually every business in Cuenca is closed. (Anyone who doubts that the Lord giveth and the Lord taketh away, sometimes in reverse order, should note that just a few years later, equally by accident, we fetched up in Ecuador during the only week of the entire year when *fanesca* is served.) I've spent Sundays in places where the Lord's Day Observance Society has had some impact. I've been in beach resorts off-season. But I don't think I'd ever been in a business district where so little life was stirring. "We're not talking here about a carousel-closed-until-spring situation," I said. "This is serious." Then, after our truly peaceful morning walk had revealed a richness of colonial architecture and a paucity of places to have lunch, I suddenly said, "Chinese!" There are Chinese restaurants in Ecuador—they're called *chifas*—and, judging from the business hours that Overseas Chinese keep in other places I have visited, I figured that a *chifa* in downtown Cuenca would not consider the day before the day before Shrove Tuesday a time when customers had to be turned away. In my mind, I could almost taste the dumplings, followed by a crab dish with garlic—the crab blindingly fresh even though Cuenca is miles inland. We found two *chifas*. Both of them were closed. Somehow this did not destroy my faith. Thinking back on it, I compare myself with those millenarians who went into a cave on the day they were certain that the world was going to end and emerged the next day stronger in their faith than ever. Even now, I think that if we had just walked a few blocks farther in Cuenca, we would have found it—Star Twinkles.

The irrational certainty that a superior Chinese restaurant might be found anywhere is fueled partly by the fact that I miss Chinatown when I'm away from New York—even when away from New York means being in Paris. I miss popping down there on my bike to bring back some mixed seafood soup with noodles from New Chao Chow. I miss scallion pancakes. I miss chive and egg pancakes. I miss those dishes with Chinese flowering chives at Great New York Noodletown. I miss the tension of sitting at the Triple Eight Palace for dim sum, wondering whether it's safe to dash over to the station where a woman is frying doughy leek dumplings—the danger being that while I'm away, carrying the check that has to be stamped for each dish, the cart with shrimp wrapped in rice noodles is going to pass our table unhailed.

But Paris! Is someone who has been willing to try the patience of his traveling companions in Cornwall by looking for the slightly better Cornish pasty prepared to say that there is nothing in Paris that might merit his efforts? Not exactly. In Paris, I do enjoy bistros and neighborhood restaurants and market food. Partway through the entrée of a three-star restaurant,

I have to admit, I often find myself thinking that, although it's certainly admirable that the chef is able to do this sort of thing, I'm not actually having a whole lot of fun. I also can't seem to help wondering, when my mind wanders between forkfuls in that sort of place, whether God really intended all that to be done to food.

In other words, I like eating in Paris, but it's not an affair of the heart. When I hear praise of some chef's *blanquette de veau,* my pulse doesn't quicken the way it might at a reference to, say, crab with cellophane noodles, ginger, garlic, and lemongrass. That was one of the dishes mentioned in a letter I got from an American resident of Paris not long before Alice and I happened to be heading in that direction on a trip that would also take us to Prague. The writer of the letter, David Jaggard, said that he and his wife—Nancy Li, a San Franciscan of Cantonese origin whose skills included the ability to read the wall signs in Chinese restaurants—had, after some years of wide-ranging and assiduous research, found a Chinese place on the Avenue de Choisy that met their standards. I was attracted not just by the dishes mentioned—Spicy Squid and Shrimp with XO Cognac Sauce was another one—but by the tone of the letter. Jaggard described himself as a composer and his wife as "a journalist and part-time counterrevolutionary." I'd written back right away saying that Chinese food in Paris was just the sort of thing I had in mind.

I could remember a time when even the most fanatic consumer of Asian food knew that in Paris he'd have to pretty much make do with the cuisine of France. Then, in the middle eighties, in the outdoor markets of Provence, I detected signs of the phenomenon I think of as the silver lining of colonialism—

the same silver lining that made Indonesian food routine in the Netherlands and brought Indian restaurants early on to English towns that would otherwise have had to muddle through with bangers and mash. (In fact, I've read that British tourist authorities, after some research, have declared the English national dish to be curry.) At the ends of cheese purveyors' cases at those weekly markets in France, I began to spot, not far from the displays of small chèvres at various stages of ripeness, Vietnamese spring rolls—vegetables and maybe shrimp wrapped in a soft skin that was, in turn, wrapped in a large mint leaf. Eventually, an outdoor market in the South of France was likely to have a separate stand or two for Vietnamese specialties, and the prepared food displayed in the food hall of, say, the Bon Marché department store in Paris included spring rolls as a matter of course, the way an English food hall would include a colonial silver lining like stuffed paratha. On Paris evenings when we'd decided to eat in the neighborhood while staying at a friend's place on the Left Bank, I often found myself walking not toward one of the local bistros but toward a rather elegant Vietnamese place called Tra Dinh, noted not only for its noodles but for the Pomerol selection in its wine cellar.

Partly because of the ease of movement within the European Community, the diversity of restaurants in large European cities eventually went well beyond their colonial pasts. When we were visiting London in the late nineties, the restaurants we thought about going to one evening with an American friend who lives there included not just Indian but Italian and Lebanese and North African. He asked us to meet him instead at a chophouse he had become fond of, explaining that he'd been conducting some business with executives of football clubs, and the football types liked the chophouse partly because "they say it has the only menu in London they can understand." Even the local specialties in European cities are no longer without foreign influence: the last fish-and-chips joint I particularly liked in London turned out to be owned by a Greek whose fish batter was made from matzoh meal.

Walking with Alice on the Left Bank of Paris one day as lunch approached, I passed places featuring not just Vietnamese noodles but Israeli falafel and North African *merlu*ᵶ and Japanese sushi and American barbecue. The effect was disorienting. "You know what would hit the spot right now?" I heard myself saying. "A burrito. Not one of those yuppie burritos. A real pulled-chicken burrito, from a place that also sells a lot of menudo."

"You're in France," Alice reminded me. "This is Paris, France."

"You're right, of course," I said. "I almost forgot the big Chinese meal we're having this evening."

As it turned out, Nancy Li, who is indeed active in the pro-democracy movement that reached its apogee in Tienanmen Square, had discovered the restaurant in question while doing some translating for a Hong Kong film producer who traveled with his own bottle of XO sauce, a condiment that some residents of Hong Kong apparently find it comforting to carry around wherever they go, in the way that people in some other cities find it comforting to carry around a container of Mace. From the fact that the place was called Sinorama ("Nobody's perfect," Jaggard noted in his letter), I had expected something slick, but Sinorama turned out to be the sort of plain, crowded, noisy joint that I have frequented in New York's Chinatown over the years. The walls were covered with signs in Chinese writing—signs whose China-town equivalents drive me mad, since they feed my suspicion that Chinese customers are getting succulent dishes I don't even know about—and Nancy Li was hardly seated before she was translating like mad. The signs did not show a strong effort at marketing, she informed me; one of the first dishes she came across was something called Big Intestines in Salty Water.

There were six of us, and, under my prodding not to forget that we were all pretty hungry, Nancy ordered deep-fried tofu skins, Chinese celery with crabs, haricots verts with XO sauce, Empire's Favorite Concubine Chicken, shrimp with cellophane noodles, stuffed bitter cucumber, Shanghai thick noodles, sticky rice pastry, and more Tsingtao beer than I'd have thought we'd be able to get down. The food was terrific. The bill was more or less the equivalent of a Manhattan Chi-natown bill—what you can imagine the meter showing at some of the fancier eateries in Paris around the time the bus-boy brings your bread and butter.

We emerged from Sinorama into a lovely fall evening. "Ah, Paris," I said as we all strolled down the Avenue de Choisy toward a taxi rank. "There is nothing like Paris and moonlight and Shanghai thick noodles."

Prague has the sort of culinary reputation that London endured in years past—a place where a traveler might seek out foreign restaurants in a desperate attempt to avoid what the natives are eating. On the plane, I armed myself with at least two fantasies about wandering into a remarkable Asian restaurant in Prague. In the first, the People's Republic of

China, as a fraternal gesture during the time Czechoslovakia was under hard-line Communist rule, had opened a fabulous Chinese restaurant in Prague, and after the revolution in 1989, the chefs had defected in order to do even more wondrous food as the blessings of the free market brought them ingredients they'd only dreamed about under Communism. In the second, North Vietnamese who had come during the war to train in Czechoslovakia had remained to open restaurants superior even to those the South Vietnamese had opened in places like Orange County, California, and Arlington, Virginia. The North Vietnamese won the war, after all; why wouldn't they also cook better?

To my astonishment, the premises of both fantasies turned out to correspond with fact. The Chinese government really had opened a restaurant in Prague in the fifties but had apparently begun to lose interest in its quality after Czechoslovakia lined up with Moscow in the split between China and the Soviet Union. So many Vietnamese had remained in Czechoslovakia after the war that they had come to constitute the country's third largest ethnic group, but they seemed to channel their entrepreneurial energy not toward restaurants but toward selling dry goods at outdoor markets. The grimness of the real situation had been reflected in an e-mail I'd received before my trip from Benjamin Widiss, a young man who had lived in Prague for a couple of years after graduating from college in the same class as Abigail. Asked about Chinese restaurants, Benj dredged up fond memories of a stand near an outlying subway stop; its egg rolls had helped sustain him through the long Czech winter. He referred to the only other Chinese restaurant he could recall as "the MSG place."

When I got in touch with Michael Kaufman—a well-traveled foreign correspondent who was then in Prague editing a magazine on Central and Eastern European affairs—he said there was a Czech specialty he wanted me to try. We drove out to a place called Restaurace U Cejpů (as far as I can tell, the little marks above letters in Czech are there to remind you that nothing is pronounced anything like it is spelled). The menu was extensive, but the category of Specialties had only two dishes listed—"Roast Pork Knee with Mustard, Horseradish, and Cabbage Salad" and "Roast Pork Knee for Big Eaters with Mustard, Horseradish, and Cabbage Salad." They were out of the first specialty. In appearance, the big eaters' specialty turned out to resemble what might happen if you managed to roast a sixteen-inch softball on the bone. "It's delicious," I said to Kaufman, quite sincerely. "Maybe not something I'd like to eat every single meal, but delicious." Kaufman said that if I wanted to stick to local specialties, I'd pretty much have to eat roast pork knee every single meal; after two years in Prague, it was the only dish he'd found that seemed worth eating.

That made me eager to find Benj's egg roll stand, and Jeffrey Jowell, a friend who was in Prague with us, volunteered to join me in the search while Alice and Jeffrey's wife, Francie, found something marginally more cultural to do. I'll admit that, as a general rule, I enjoy looking for something in a strange town irrespective of what it is—particularly if the search requires a ride on the subway. Also, the subway stop Benj had mentioned, Budějovická, also happened to be near a Chinese restaurant called Čínské Zátiší, which both Kaufman and one of the guidebooks had touted as Prague's best. It's always advisable to have a fallback. Miraculously, we found the egg roll stand, still functioning four or five years after Benj had gone off to graduate school in California; it was, just as he'd remembered, next to a pet store, which was named Zoo Benny. The egg rolls were no match for the spring rolls I'd had in Avignon and Vaison-la-Romaine a few weeks before, but they weren't bad. I liked imagining Benj and his pals, desperate for something decent to eat, wolfing down egg rolls while watching the rats play in the window of Zoo Benny. When I spotted Čínské Zátiší just across the street, I decided we should treat the egg rolls as an hors d'oeuvre. A couple of dishes at Čínské Zátiší were first-rate—dumplings that had no resemblance to the Czech dumplings I've heard described as "what you'd expect stale bread to taste like," for instance. Jeffrey said that they were among the best dumplings he'd ever had. He seemed to like them even better than the Roast Pork Knee for Big Eaters with Mustard, Horseradish, and Cabbage Salad we'd had the day before. Also, as we polished off dishes like Hacked Chicken and Dan-Dan Noodles, the restaurant started filling up with Chinese customers. Soon, there were forty or fifty of them, and we were about the only Westerners left. Could it be, I wondered, that the Chinese and the Czechs, both now devoted to the free market, were pals again and Beijing has sent over a huge delegation to decide where to reopen the restaurant of my fantasies? Maybe. Meanwhile, though, I started worrying that I was missing some dishes that the Chinese were negotiating for in their own language—maybe something as exotic as Big Intestines in Salty Water. Where was Nancy Li when I needed her? The feeling of missing out on some of the best dishes made me think longingly of New York's Chinatown. I was about ready to go home.

9.

THE RED AND THE WHITE

≡

Before we get onto the question of whether experienced wine drinkers can actually tell the difference between red wine and white, I should probably tell you a little something about my background in the field. I have never denied that when I'm trying to select a bottle of wine in a liquor store I'm strongly influenced by the picture on the label. (I like a nice mountain, preferably in the middle distance.) And, yes, I did once write in a newspaper column that in a discussion comparing French and American varietals I was the one who remarked that Château Lafite-Rothschild and Manischewitz Pink Cream Catawba "both tasted rather Jewish." In writing that, I should add, I was only trying to make a little joke; I've never been in a discussion comparing French and American varietals.

When I was growing up, in Kansas City, I didn't know about people drinking wine at meals that were not being eaten

in celebration of a major anniversary. I assume that my neighbors would have been as startled as I to hear about such
carrying on. Years later, after I'd moved to New York, a newspaperman in my hometown did me a great favor, and when I
wondered aloud what I could get for him, a friend of mine in
New York—a sophisticated friend of mine who considered
himself something of a gourmet, now that I think of it—said
that a case of wine was always appreciated. I phoned the
newspaperman's son-in-law in Kansas City to ask if he could
find out, discreetly, what sort of wine was particularly fancied
in his in-laws' house, and the son-in-law got back to me with a
question of his own: "Does Wild Turkey count?" Even now, I
can't imagine many people in Kansas City, Missouri, routinely
opening a bottle of Merlot at dinnertime—any more than I
can imagine them eating Seared Maine Diver Sea Scallops or
Poached Pavé of Arctic Char with Cider-Braised Fennel or
Leek and Fava Bean Risotto. These days, I do drink wine
more often than the adults I knew in my boyhood did. Still, if
I'm at a meal at which drink orders are being given by the
glass, I am likely to say to the waiter, "What sort of fancy beer
do you have on tap?"

I have spent a certain amount of time in the company of
wine cognoscenti, but I wouldn't claim that I have distinguished myself on those occasions. Many years ago, for
instance, a wine maker I know was kind enough to invite
me to the "barrel tasting" of California wines that used to be
held annually at the Four Seasons restaurant in New York—
an event that was considered a very hot ticket in the wine
game. At the table, many glasses of wine were put in front of
us. Then, someone who had his mouth very close to the

microphone talked about each wine in what I believe scholars would call excruciating detail—the type of vines that had been grafted together to produce it, for instance, and how long it had been in stainless steel vats or oak barrels. Displaying manners that I thought would have made my mother proud, I drank what was placed before me—not noticing, as I glanced around to see whether more food was ever going to appear, that everyone else was just sipping. I have since heard two or three versions of what transpired that evening, but they do not differ in whether or not I fell asleep at the table. (According to one version, the last polite question I mumbled to my host was, "And then you graft the vines onto the stainless steel vats?") Particularly considering my performance at the Four Seasons that evening, it's perfectly possible that some people asked to sum up my knowledge of and attitude toward wine might respond "ignorance, tempered slightly by philistinism."

On the other hand, I have, in a manner of speaking, worked in the wine industry for a number of years. An old friend of mine named Bruce Neyers makes wine in the Napa Valley. I think it would be too much to say that I'm an adviser to Bruce in his business, unless suggesting that he put a mountain on his label counts. Thanks to the miracle of the fax machine, though, I act as a sort of volunteer copy editor of the announcements that he sends out to his regular customers—what people in the trade would call his offering letters. Bruce, a wry man who grew up in Wilmington, Delaware, and assumed through college that he would spend his life as a research chemist for DuPont, tends to discuss wine in straightforward terms even when he's addressing the sort of wine fiends who do close readings of offering letters. Still, I can't claim that I know precisely what he means when he writes, say, "The malolactic fermentation went to completion." What I bring to my editing task is not expertise in viticulture but a long experience in such matters as comma placement.

If Bruce shows up at my house during a business trip to New York, he is usually carrying some wine, a custom that reflects both his natural generosity and his concern about what he otherwise might be forced to drink. He has never considered my scenery selection strategy a completely satisfactory way to build a cellar. He has particularly grim memories of a Chardonnay that attracted me with a view of mountains that are apparently near enough the grape-growing region of the Hungarian Danube to be depicted in the middle distance. He doesn't ask in advance if I'd prefer red or white—presumably because he knows that the question would give me the opportunity to say, "But can anybody really tell the difference?"

Why? Because, as best I can remember, it was from Bruce or one of his acquaintances in the Napa Valley that I first heard about the color test given at the University of California at Davis, whose department of viticulture and enology is renowned in the wine world. I got the impression that the test was often given to visitors from the wine industry, but since this was back in the early eighties, such details are hazy. I was definitely told, though, that the folks at Davis poured wine that was at room temperature into black glasses—thus removing the temperature and color cues that are a large part of what people assume is taste—and that the tasters often couldn't tell red wine from white. After Bruce returned from a short course at Davis in the mid-seventies, he had someone at the Joseph Phelps winery, where he then worked, set up a red-white test with black glasses. Bruce got three out of five.

I suppose I am programmed to expect that sort of result. I was raised by a man who, although he had never tasted coffee in his life, once told me that blindfolded I couldn't tell the difference between coffee with milk and coffee without milk. It has never occurred to me that the software drummers who are in the habit of saying to the bartender "J & B on the rocks" or "Ketel One with a twist" might actually be able to recognize their favorite brands of booze in a blind tasting. In the seventies, my friend Jeffrey Jowell, who has a farm in the west of England, began raising chickens and boasting of the gloriously distinctive taste of their eggs. When I arrived for a visit, I secretly replaced the freshly gathered eggs in his larder with eggs from a London supermarket, and I try to remind him at least semiannually that he raved about the next omelet to come out of the kitchen. In temperament and genes as well as in geographic origin, I'm from the Show-Me state.

For years, I was likely to mention the Davis test whenever the subject of wine connoisseurship came up, even if I happened to be drinking a glass of beer at the time. A couple of years ago, for instance, a pleasant young man who was showing us around a winery owned by an acquaintance of mine in New York State mentioned that, as part of his final year at the Culinary Institute of America—the institution food people are referring to when they mention the CIA—he had gone to Davis for a wine course. Naturally, I asked him how he did on The Test. He changed the subject. But at the end of the tour, after we'd all downed a friendly glass of wine or two and become better acquainted, he suddenly turned to me and said, quietly, "I got three out of seven."

In 1994 I mentioned the test in *The New Yorker* in the course of discussing the discovery that Sigmund Freud's seduction theory was based on data he had fudged. Talking about what lay ahead for the Freudians, I posited the question as the Davis Conundrum—how to deal with information that may appear to call into question a tenet that is central to a system of belief. Putting the Conundrum in terms of the Davis test itself, I wrote, "Does the failure to distinguish red from white undercut all the learned talk you hear about body and vintage and integrity and which side of the hill the grapes came from?"

I know what you're thinking: Isn't it rather snide to use a phrase like "which side of the hill the grapes came from" while talking about whether wine drinkers can actually tell red from white? Is it possible that a self-confessed beer-swilling ignoramus got interested in the Davis test simply as a way of debunking wine connoisseurship? As another wine business friend of mine likes to point out, wine is way beyond any other subject in inspiring in the American layman an urge to refute the notion of expertise. (Modern art must come in second.) I'd like to think that I'm above that sort of thing. I took it for granted, I'd like to think, that experts could explain not only why certain red wines and certain white wines would be difficult for even a connoisseur to tell apart but also why this did not call into question the legitimacy of wine expertise— and could do so, if necessary, in excruciating detail.

It's not as if wine connoisseurship lacks informed criticism from people who are not beer-swilling ignoramuses. Mark Dornan of the Beverage Testing Institute, for instance, says to anyone who asks him that rating wines on a scale of a hundred, which is now common practice, is "utterly pseudoscientific." Tim Hanni, a master of wines, believes that most commentary about wines fails to take into account the biological individuality of consumers; he claims that he can predict what sort of wine appeals to you according to such factors as how heavily you salt your food and whether your mother suffered a lot from morning sickness while carrying you. Hanni has said for years that the matching of a particular color of wine with a particular food is a scam, there being "absolutely no premise historically, culturally, or biologically for drinking red wine with meat." As a way of illustrating the role played by anticipation in taste, Frederic Brochet, a researcher with the enology faculty of the University of Bordeaux, asked some experts to describe two wines that appeared by their labels to be a distinguished *grand cru classe* and a cheap table wine—actually, Brochet had refilled both bottles with a third, midlevel wine—and found his subjects mightily impressed by the supposed *grand cru* and dismissive of the same wine when it was in the *vin ordinaire* bottle.

An urge to refute the notion of expertise certainly did seem to be reflected in the headline of an article in *The Times* of London about the research Brochet had been carrying on: CHEEKY LITTLE TEST EXPOSES WINE "EXPERTS" AS WEAK AND FLAT. The headline caught the tone of the article, by Adam Sage, which began, "Drinkers have long suspected it, but now French researchers have finally proved it: wine 'experts' know no more than the rest of us." The test of Brochet's that caught my eye consisted partly of asking wine drinkers to describe what appeared to be a red wine and a white wine. They were, in fact, two glasses of the same white wine, one of which had been colored red with flavorless and odorless dye. The comments about the "red" wine used what people in the trade call red-wine descriptors. "It is a well known psychological phenomenon—you taste what you're expecting to taste," said Brochet in *The Times.* "They were expecting to taste a red wine and so they did. . . . About two or three percent of people detect the white wine flavour, but invariably they have little experience of wine culture. Connoisseurs tend to fail to do so. The more training they have, the more mistakes they make because they are influenced by the color of the wine."

Reading about Brochet's color experiment revived my interest in the Davis test. I was curious, for one thing, about whether there was a way to compare his results with the results the Davis people had collected over the years—although, as I understood it, the Davis testers, working in the straightforward tradition of the American West, actually told a subject that he was choosing between red and white rather than trying to sneak a bottle of adulterated white past him. I decided it might be time, after all these years, to visit Davis and collect some statistics on what the test actually showed. I got the Department of Viticulture and Enology on the telephone and explained my interest to a friendly woman there who is employed to field inquiries from people like me. She told me that as far as she knew Davis had never conducted such a test.

"Imagine that!" Bruce Neyers said, when I told him of my chat with the folks at Davis. He found it unsurprising that an institution with an interest in the distinctions among wines would have difficulty recalling evidence that the most elementary distinction can often not be made. Like a lot of wine people I've spoken to about the test over the years, Bruce thinks it would be easy enough to pick out some unusual wines that might muddy the difference between the taste of red and white—that is presumably what was done in the test he'd taken that time at Phelps—but even a loaded test might be pounced on as evidence that the judgments of wine experts are, as Adam Sage put it in his *Times* of London piece, "little more than self-delusion." When I asked Bruce if he could round up some Napa Valley wine people to take the red-white test, assuming I couldn't track it down at Davis, he said they might want to remain anonymous, since there were probably better ways to begin a wine industry résumé than "Although I can't distinguish red wine from white wine . . ."

If anybody at Davis knew about a red-white test, I'd been told, it would probably be Ann Noble, who, when I dropped in to see her, was just winding up a twenty-eight-year teaching career in the Department of Viticulture and Enology. Professor Noble's field is taste and smell, particularly smell. She has noted that as children we are taught to label colors but not smells. In an effort to correct that oversight, she not only conducted in her courses what she calls "a kindergarten of the nose" but also invented the Wine Aroma Wheel, which permits someone to describe the aroma of a wine in specific terms and to identify varietals by their smell. Someone with an aroma wheel knows, for instance, that a Pinot Noir can be distinguished from a Zinfandel because it has the smell of berry, berry jam (strawberry), vanilla, butter, and spiciness rather than the smell of berry, black pepper, raisin, soy, butter, and vanilla.

Professor Noble told me that the test I'd heard about sounded like an urban myth. She regularly tested her students at the end of the semester by giving them wine in black glasses to identify, she said. But what they were trying to name was the varietal, not the color. For a couple of years, she saved the wrong answers, and she found that perhaps ten to fifteen percent of them were not simply the wrong varietal but a wrong varietal that also was the wrong color. Conceivably, it occurred to me, that test could have been embellished over the years to become the Davis red-white test I'd heard about, although ten or fifteen percent amounted to a lot fewer wrong answers than I would have expected. Then Professor Noble told me that in the tests she gave her students they were, of course, reaching their conclusions by smell alone.

"Smell alone?" I said.

"This is only by smell," she said. "The minute you put it in your mouth, it's game over. The difference is night and day."

She could imagine some wines that would be less obvious—Beaujolais, for instance, has less tannin than most red wines—but basically she thought that the astringency of red wine would be a giveaway if you were allowed to taste as well as smell. She offered to demonstrate on the spot, and after ducking across the hall into her lab, she returned with two wines in black glasses for me to taste. I tried both of them, and then I said, "The first one was red and the second one was white."

Professor Noble seemed taken aback. "It was the other way around," she said.

She was kind enough to come up with some mitigating circumstances. "It could have been test anxiety," she said. Then she tasted the wines and added, "I should have gotten a different red wine. This is not as astringent as I thought." Then she said that the red was, in fact, a weird wine, from Georgia. She didn't mean Georgia as in Tbilisi, where wine consumption is among the highest in the world; she meant Georgia as in Waycross. Then she mentioned that I hadn't had a warm-up taste.

I tried to help her think of other excuses. I told her the sun was in my eyes. I thought I'd reserve my other standard excuse—the ball hit a pebble—just in case she suggested that we do the test again.

Professor Noble said she'd ask around among other faculty members whose courses were most likely to have included a red-white test, but by the weekend of the test Bruce Neyers had agreed to set up, she had e-mailed me that no one at Davis seemed to know about such a test. (Neither, it later turned out, did the people in charge of the Culinary Institute of America's six-week California course that our winery guide had apparently been referring to.) By chance, both of my sons-in-law, Brian and Alex, were in San Francisco that weekend, and they were willing to act as tasters. Both of them have some interest in wine. My daughters, neither of whom drinks much wine, opted out; when we discussed the test over dinner in San Francisco the night before we were to drive up to Bruce's house, Sarah said that the sort of wine descriptors she would use if asked to taste two wines might be "yucky" and "yuckier." Both of my sons-in-law seemed pretty free of test anxiety.

"I'm not worried about failing," Alex said, partway through dinner. "I'm worried about failing and Brian passing."

Rather than repeat the sort of test he'd taken years before, Bruce had avoided wines he considered particularly likely to fool the tasters; he had gathered eight French wines that he thought of as typical products of the grapes they'd been made from. Not wanting to skew the results, I didn't mention to Brian and Alex what Ann Noble had told me about the way to increase your odds—take about three sips instead of one, building up the astringency of the tannin if it's red wine to produce a drying sensation in your mouth that she thought would be hard to miss. As Bruce stood where he couldn't be observed and poured the wine into black glasses, he said that a couple of visiting wine retailers from Springfield, Missouri, known in my home state as Gateway to the Ozarks, had dropped in just before we arrived and identified eight out of eight wines. Although he insisted he was telling the truth, I figured he was trying to make Brian and Alex nervous with some sort of Napa Valley version of trash talk, and I tried to keep them calm. "I want you to know that I'm totally even-handed on this," I said to them. "Either one of you guys can be humiliated. I don't care which one it is."

As it turned out, they both did pretty well. Each person, wearing sunglasses as an additional security measure, was asked to go through the wines twice—first trying to identify the color by smell, then by taste. Alex got seven out of eight both times. Brian got only four by taste, but he got six by smell. By taste, both of them misidentified as white a Sancerre Rouge made from Pinot Noir grapes in the Loire Valley. That was also one of two wines misidentified when tasted by another guest, Larry Bain, a San Francisco restaurant proprietor considered by Bruce to be knowledgeable in enological matters—which means that if your brother-in-law is particularly arrogant about the sophistication of his palate, you might consider keeping a bottle of Reverdy Sancerre rouge on hand, along with a black glass and a pair of sunglasses.

And what other information did the test at Bruce's provide? Taking an average of the three participants I witnessed—if Bruce's earlier guests really were from Missouri, they will understand that I can't count anything I didn't see with my own eyes—I concluded that experienced wine drinkers can tell red from white by taste about seventy percent of the time, as long as the test is being administered by someone who isn't interested in trying to fool them. That made me wonder whether there were similar statistics somewhere in a file drawer in Davis. If The Test never existed, after all, how did the *New Yorker* fact checker verify it in 1994? Even assuming there was some lapse in the legendary thoroughness of the fact-checking department, why didn't the authorities at Davis write to deny the existence of the Davis Conundrum? And if no test existed, what test was that young man who showed us around the New York State winery taking when he got three out of seven? I sometimes ponder these questions, when I listen to wine talk while sipping the amber microbrew the waiter brought when I asked him if he had any fancy beers on tap. At least I think it's an amber microbrew.

10.

POSOLE DREAMS

—
—

I want you to know that when I had the idea of opening a Northern New Mexican restaurant in Manhattan, I was way ahead of the curve. This was, after all, in 1971. I had returned to New York after a summer in New Mexico, much of it spent in the high desert country from Santa Fe north. Northern New Mexico is well known as a singularly beautiful place that has always been an inspiration to people of artistic bent— Georgia O'Keeffe and D. H. Lawrence, for instance, not to speak of generations of eastern remittance men who, gazing out of their exquisitely restored adobe houses toward the surrounding mountains, must be moved now and then to compose deeply felt poetry on the subject of their trust funds. (I once heard a man in Taos explain the origins of the Santa Fe Anglo community by what he called the Theory of the Dumbest Sons. According to this theory, there was a time when a number of wealthy eastern families assigned their dumbest son—the son who was of no use in the bank or the factory— to a life of coupon clipping in Santa Fe, an agreeable and relatively exotic spot, and everything that has happened since can be traced to either the customs or the genes brought from the East by those thick founding offspring. Fortunately, these are not the folks who do the cooking.) Once settled in the stunning scenery of Santa Fe and the counties that extend north toward the Colorado line, people who might not have been particularly arty in Chicago or Buffalo may take up a paintbrush or acquire a portfolio of photographs of Pueblo pottery. After just a couple of months in New Mexico, I myself had been inspired to hatch a scheme for creating a steady source of quality posole in Manhattan.

Posole is made by boiling corn kernels in a lime solution (lime as in limestone, not lime as in the juice you have in the margaritas you drink while you're waiting for your posole) and then drying them. It is often served in a bowl as a sort of stew, with the addition of pork or chicken and chiles. It has an earthy taste, and a texture that can make you forget your troubles. In Northern New Mexican homes, posole is traditionally served during the Christmas season. My restaurant scheme was based on the desire to eat it every day of the year.

In 1971, of course, the restaurant scene in New York was not terribly open to the introduction of new American regional cuisines. When residents of Manhattan thought of American regions, they simply divided the country in two— New York and Out of Town—and, unsurprisingly, there were not a lot of restaurants that featured out-of-towners' cuisine. Restaurant menus did not then boast about having acquired their mussels from Puget Sound or their morels from Michigan; the menu word that justified tacking an extra couple of dollars on the entrée was still *imported*. Louisiana Cajuns, shoveling down crawfish and boudin and tasso and crabs the way they always had, were blissfully unaware that, through no fault of their own, they would someday become associated on New York menus with burnt fish. Chez Panisse had just barely opened its doors in Berkeley; if a restaurant in New York had included the word *California* in its name, the public would have expected a drive-in with blond carhops. Imagine the impact on this scene if someone had opened a Northern New Mexican restaurant called Taos County.

That's right: the name of the restaurant was to be Taos County. That would set it apart from Mexican restaurants— although in 1971, long before New York finally got a serious wave of immigration from the area around Puebla, there weren't that many Mexican restaurants in Manhattan to set it apart from. The name hinted at the decor. I'm pretty sure, though, that my original vision of the decor has become adulterated over the years by images that I acquired later: what I see now when I think of Taos County looks uncomfortably like one of those exquisitely restored adobe houses inhabited by the remittance men, or maybe a little like an advertisement for the Southwest Collection of Ralph Lauren Home Furnishings.

On the walls, there are huge photographs of Indian pueblos and the Sangre de Cristo Mountains and the adobe churches in villages like Truchas and Las Trampas—villages that, years before anyone had thought of writing the Declaration of Independence, were established by Spanish-speaking *pobladores,* or settlers, who must have turned their attention almost immediately to figuring out creative ways to use blue corn. (The cuisine that emerged from the blending of Spanish and Indian traditions is sometimes said to have been based on "corn, beans, squash, and chile—and not all that much squash.") The floors of Taos County, as I can still see them, have stunning rugs from Chimayo, woven by descendants of the people who brought weaving to the Navajos. In the niches of the walls and in glass cases are Pueblo artifacts and maybe a few santos. The furniture is the color of Northern New Mexican buttes, unless those things are mesas.

That's not exactly the look of restaurants in Northern New Mexico that are likely to have a decent bowl of posole. They tend toward rough wood and exposed beams. In fact, the possibility once occurred to me that posole wouldn't come out right in a restaurant whose beams are covered, in the way that mayonnaise is said not to thicken properly if there's a thunderstorm approaching. Whatever the design of Taos County was, I remember being confident that it would knock the critics dead, even before they had a chance to bite into a sopaipilla or taste a blue corn tamale covered with green chile. At least that's what I kept telling an acquaintance of mine I'll call Irwin—the person I was hoping to persuade to launch Taos County. No, I wasn't going to do the restaurant myself. I'm more of an idea man. I just wanted a place to eat.

Irwin, who left the city not many years later, was then in real estate. He had acquired control of a building he was turning into co-op apartments, and he was trying to decide what sort of restaurant he wanted in the commercial space on the ground floor. Taos County, I kept telling him. Nobody in New York had tasted posole. Nobody had tasted sopaipillas.

Nobody was familiar with the pure pleasure that a chile fancier in Santa Fe gets from settling in at the counter—yes, in that era before sushi bars had made counter eating respectable in upmarket New York restaurants, Taos County was going to have a counter where you could eat like a gent, the way Musso & Frank's in Hollywood or Tadich Grill in San Francisco had counters where you could eat like a gent—and say, "Give me a bowl of green" or "I'll have the enchilada with red."

I think Irwin, who was not a traveler, had New Mexican food mixed up in his mind with Tex-Mex food. I tried to explain to him that even though New Mexican cooking did include some of the dishes Americans were used to finding in Mexican restaurants—tamales, for instance, and chiles rellenos, and enchiladas—those dishes had a different taste than the Tex-Mex equivalents, particularly if they were turned out by a cook who had the touch with a green or a red. Once New Yorkers tasted the difference, I told Irwin, he'd have to hire large men with electric cattle prods to control the crowds clamoring to get in. As I remember how all of this turned out, Irwin opened a steak joint in the building instead.

"Posole!" I said to myself, as the plane I had caught in Chicago touched down on a cold day one winter many years later. I thought for a moment that, in my excitement, I had said it out loud. Some of the passengers around me were, in fact, muttering to themselves loudly enough to be heard, and some of what they muttered was not polite. An ice storm having kept our plane from landing in Kansas City, the flight had continued on to its next stop—Albuquerque, New Mexico. A few minutes before, I'd been disappointed about having to bypass Kansas City. Since the plane had taken off from Chicago, at about six that morning, I'd been overcome with hometown barbecue nostalgia, and I'd begun charting out the logistics involved in punctuating my appointments that day with lunch at two or three of the rib purveyors my Kansas City friend Fats Goldberg used to refer to, with affection born out of long patronage, as greasepits.

Now, though, I was thinking about posole. For a decade or so after my dreams of Taos County were dashed by Irwin's insistence that a good porterhouse was just what Manhattan needed, I had visited Northern New Mexico now and then. But as that plane arrived in Albuquerque unexpectedly, I realized that I hadn't been in what I still thought of as posole country for twenty years. The barbecue nostalgia had already evaporated. I phoned Dave Grusin and Nan Newton, friends of mine who live in Santa Fe, and asked them if they were busy for lunch.

An hour or so later, I was in Santa Fe, and Dave and Nan and I were sitting at a pleasant restaurant called Cafe San Estevan, which does a somewhat upscale version of Northern New Mexican cuisine. I was eating a bowl of quality posole. I didn't even notice what Dave and Nan were eating. I was at peace. I had been chased by a storm since early that morning—a storm that first threatened to shut the airport in Chicago, then did shut down virtually the entire city of Kansas City, and, from what I'd heard on the car radio on the ride up from the airport, was now approaching Albuquerque—but I was, at least for the moment, unconcerned.

With my posole, I had an order of sopaipillas. I don't think I've ever had sopaipillas anywhere but in New Mexico. *The*

Santa Fe School of Cooking Cookbook describes them as "puffy, golden 'sofa pillows' of deep fried leavened dough." I think of them as popovers that have fallen in with a fast crowd. A lot of restaurants in Northern New Mexico keep honey on the table to put on sopaipillas. Old-time residents sometimes explain to visitors that sopaipillas with honey are used during a meal to blunt the impact of particularly hot chile—the way that parents in the English countryside explain to their children that nature always provides dock weed near stinging nettles because an application of dock weed will soothe the sting. Cafe San Estevan happens to make particularly airy sopaipillas. I had to run for the airport before the storm caught up with me, but I told Dave and Nan that I'd be back.

"Could I have forgotten about carne adovada?" I was saying to Dave and Nan. "Or is it possible that I somehow didn't know about carne adovada? Is it possible that knowledge of carne adovada was, for some reason, kept from me—and that I therefore lost an untold number of opportunities to eat carne adovada?" This outburst took place three or four months after I'd been sheltered from the storm at Cafe San Estevan. A few hours before, I had finally made it back to Santa Fe, and I was having dinner with Dave and Nan at Maria's. Although Maria's features a hundred margaritas and has a rack in the foyer filled with brochures of local tourist attractions and employs a trio of strolling Mexican musicians, it nonetheless remains for residents of Santa Fe a dependable specialist in Northern New Mexican food. My intention was simple: I was going to eat enough of such food to hold me for a while.

Since my diversion to Albuquerque, I had made some efforts to find an outpost of posole country in Manhattan. After all, I figured, a lot had happened in the New York restaurant business in the past thirty years. My efforts had not met with success. One of the places I'd heard about, Los Dos Molinos, seemed to have been designed for citizens who have gotten about ten years past spring break at Daytona Beach but had not lost their taste for specialties like a "Kick Ass Pitcher" of margaritas. Although the red and green chile served as a dip with the chips would have been perfectly recognizable to a New Mexico purist, he might have been put off by his first glance at the menu. Sopaipillas were listed under desserts. In the most serious deviation from the gospel, the red and the green were identified on the menu as *chili*—a spelling that would make any New Mexican connoisseur shudder. Chili is what people in Texas and California eat at chili contests and, to the astonishment of people from Northern New Mexico, even in between chili contests—chopped meat and chili powder and maybe beans. It has no relation to a bowl of New Mexican red or green, which is somewhere in the neighborhood of a sauce or a soup or a stew, perhaps with a few pieces of meat in it, and is spelled *chile*. I was reminded of the time my younger daughter and I set out to check the authenticity of American-style hamburgers in Paris and found that the first place we went to on the Champs-Elysées served burgers that were rectangular rather than round: There's an urge to pull the proprietors aside and say, "Guys, we've got some pretty basic work to do here."

The other restaurant that seemed to have a connection to New Mexico was a grill on the Upper East Side called Canyon

Road—presumably named after the street in Santa Fe that is known for its art galleries. At Canyon Road, *chile* was spelled in the New Mexican manner (as in a "goat cheese and poblano chile" quesadilla) but, by New Mexico standards, there wasn't any. Although it had the faux adobe interior and exposed beams often found in Santa Fe, Canyon Road—like Los Dos Molinos, which is part of a small Arizona-based chain— turned out to be more of a southwestern restaurant than a Northern New Mexican restaurant. Neither Canyon Road nor Los Dos Molinos had posole on the menu, and I had the feeling that it wouldn't do me any good to return to either of them during Christmas season and check again.

Nan and Dave had volunteered to accompany me while I stoked up in Santa Fe and the surrounding area. Nan, though, had already asked how many straight meals of strictly New Mexican food we could manage, since it is hardly spa cuisine. As it happened, I was already a meal ahead of her by the time we sat down at Maria's: when I'd arrived in town, at two-thirty or three in the afternoon, I was famished, and I popped into a place called La Choza, where, in a funky and agreeable little garden, I'd downed a sopaipilla stuffed with pulled chicken and a fine bowl of posole.

I hadn't thought I'd be able to eat much just a few hours later, but Maria's carne adovada had changed all that. It was described on the menu as "lean and tender pork marinated in red chile, herbs, and spices and baked to perfection." If it were made crudely, I suppose, carne adovada could conjure up the possibility that your grandmother might snap one day and drench her signature brisket with hot sauce before serving it to her unsuspecting family. Made right, it retains the almost smoky taste of red chiles—which are simply green chiles that have been allowed to ripen into redness and have then been dried. I told Dave and Nan that I liked carne adovada almost as much as I liked posole. I had a bowl of posole on the side anyway. Also a bowl of green. Just in case.

At breakfast a couple of days later, I found myself comparing notes with a young man from Denver who had a mission similar to mine. He gets to Santa Fe a lot more on business than I do, but not often enough to stave off a terrible craving for New Mexican food. We had both fetched up at the community table at Tecolote Cafe—a place that's open only for breakfast and lunch. In a Northern New Mexican restaurant, of course, it's often difficult to tell the difference between breakfast and lunch; at the stand at the Albuquerque Airport specializing in the food of New Mexico, for instance, I noticed that the two dishes listed under the category of Breakfast were a breakfast burrito and carne adovada with eggs.

The Tecolote Cafe serves the same menu from 7:00 A.M. to 2:00 P.M., and has as its motto "Great Breakfast—No Toast." It's known for its green chile, in the way that La Choza and its less strictly New Mexican older cousin, The Shed, are known for their red chile. (Established restaurants in Santa Fe often have long-term contracts with specific New Mexican chile growers—usually those near Hatch, two hundred and fifty miles to the south.) My eating companion from Denver said that when he asked the advice of an old Santa Fe hand before his first trip, the friend said to go to Tecolote and "order anything you want, with the green."

Breakfast turned out to be the meal I always had on my own while I was in Santa Fe. I could picture Nan nibbling on some yoghurt and fresh fruit as she contemplated what our lunch and dinner were going to be like, but I tried not to let that spoil my appetite. In fact, one morning, as I began thinking about how few mealtimes there were before my departure compared with how many chile pits I had left to visit, I downed back-to-back breakfast burritos—first at a place near the Plaza called Tia Sophia's and then at Horseman's Haven, a café that occupies part of an abandoned filling station out toward the interstate and outfits its waitresses in T-shirts that say (justifiably, many residents think) HOTTEST CHILE IN TOWN. In both places, I had half the burrito covered in green chile and the other half covered in red—a combination that people in Santa Fe sometimes call Christmas. It beats cornflakes by a mile.

Horseman's Haven is the sort of place where you can encounter a booth full of actual horsemen, wearing the tightly woven straw hats that ranch hands in the Southwest favor, next to a booth full of people who look as if they might have arrived in the area in the early seventies to join a crafts commune. It occurred to me that a scholar of Northern New Mexican cuisine could use its menu as evidence that the cultural mingling that started hundreds of years ago with the *pobladores* and the Indians has never really stopped: The side dishes include home fries, grits, red or green chile, blue corn tortillas, and sprouts.

Not to criticize, but on my last night in Santa Fe, Nan seemed to be flagging. We were having dinner at The Shed, and I noticed that she ordered salad as an appetizer. As I tucked into the enchilada with red, I was thinking that, despite my best efforts, I hadn't eaten everything I'd come to eat. We'd had lunch at El Paragua in Española, a restaurant I remembered from the seventies, but we hadn't had a chance to eat at the highly recommended little stand next door called El Parasol. We'd had some interesting modern takes on traditional Northern New Mexican cuisine—at Cafe Pasqual's, near the Plaza, for instance—but I hadn't tried the Horseman's Haven's intriguing idea of a green chile cheeseburger. I didn't know how long it would be before I felt a terrible craving that could not be dealt with in New York. After all, despite the opportunities New Yorkers have been given in the past thirty years to sample the cuisine of almost every imaginable country and region and province and maybe even an exotic neighborhood or two, there still didn't seem to be a restaurant in Manhattan specializing in New Mexican food.

No New Mexican food in Manhattan! Where had I heard that before? Wouldn't the obvious solution to a problem like that be to launch a restaurant—a restaurant with an irresistible name, like Taos County? Thirty years later, we would still be ahead of the curve. In fact, Taos County was actually a better idea than ever: in the seventies, I hadn't even thought of including carne adovada. We'd have to tweak the decor a bit, of course, but that wouldn't be difficult. The only other problem would be tracking down Irwin.

11.

DON'T MENTION IT

≡

I suppose Kenny Shopsin, the proprietor of a small restaurant near my house in the Village, could qualify as eccentric in a number of ways, but one of his views is particularly stupefying to journalists who have had prolonged contact with proprietors of retail businesses in New York: He has always hated publicity. I've tried not to take this personally. I became a regular customer, mainly at lunch, in 1982, when Kenny and his wife, Eve, turned a grocery store they had been running on the same premises into a thirty-four-seat café. Before that, I was a regular customer of the grocery store—the sort of compact and eclectically stocked establishment that New Yorkers sometimes refer to as a corner store. The corner store was itself a bit eccentric.

Its proprietors called a lot of the customers by name, and the conversation often drew in anyone who just happened to be standing in front of the counter waiting to pay for a quart of milk or studying the canned goods along the wall to find the appropriate soup. Some of the customers had apparently been introduced by Kenny, who (sometimes as a disembodied voice from behind the meat-slicing machine) had a habit of saying, "Hey, you two might as well know each other—you're neighbors." Somehow, space had been found in the center of the store for a wooden rocking chair with a worn pad on the seat, and it was often occupied. Customers were welcome to stop at a bookshelf near the door and take or leave a paperback. Overhead, a clown could be made to cycle back and forth on a wire.

At first glance, the place seemed to have the predictable inventory—when I try to envision the inside of a New York corner store, my mind fills with walls of cat food—but on the counter were two or three plates of homemade cookies with names like Rosie's Cinnamon Butter Crunchies and Meg's Scottish Short Bread and Keen Specials. Next to the cookies was a huge jar of beans for the bean-counting contest—one of the prizes was, naturally, the beans—and next to that was our favorite of Kenny's gum ball machines. Inside its globe, a cheerful little man with a necktie and a grocer's apron stood waiting with his scoop in hand. For only a penny, he would nod, turn to the cupboard on his left, open it, withdraw a gum ball, and turning in the other direction, drop it down a chute that led to the outside world. The gum ball machines were sometimes patronized by an adult customer—someone would slap a nickel on the counter and say, out of the corner of his mouth, "Gimme five singles" or "Break this five for me"—but they were a particular draw for children. Abigail and Sarah, who were about six and three when we started patronizing what was officially called Shopsin's General Store, referred to it as the Bubble Gum Store.

When the transformation to a restaurant was made, my daughters were around junior high school age, and even when they grew up and began living out of the city, they considered Shopsin's—or Kenny's, as they started calling it—an extension of their kitchen. Usually, they would take only a brief glance at the menu—a menu that grew to include at least nine hundred items, some of them as unusual as Cotton Picker Gumbo Melt Soup or Hanoi Hoppin John with Shrimp or Bombay Turkey Cloud Sandwich or Bugaloo-Shrimp Tabbuleh & Corn Chips or Curried Rutabaga Cream Soup—and then order something that was not listed, such as "tomato soup the way Sarah likes it." Like my daughters, Ken and Eve seemed to make the transition from corner store to restaurant effortlessly. The restaurant turned out to be to restaurants what the corner store had been to corner stores, and Kenny, who had an aversion to publicity as a grocer, didn't change his attitude when he became a restaurant proprietor.

When a phone call came from a restaurant guidebook that wanted to include Shopsin's, Kenny would sometimes say that the place was no longer in operation, identifying himself as the workman who had come to move out the fixtures. Sometime in the eighties, a persistent English guidebook carried a generally complimentary review of Shopsin's that started with a phrase like "Although it has no decor . . ." Eve expressed outrage, not simply at the existence of the review but also at its content. "Do you call this 'no decor'?" she demanded of me one evening when I was there having an early supper—the only sort of supper available at Shopsin's, which hadn't strayed far from grocery store hours. She waved her arm to take in the entire restaurant.

I looked around. Shopsin's still looked a lot like a corner store. It had an old pressed-tin ceiling. There were shelves, left over from the grocery store, that were always piled high and not terribly neatly with ingredients and supplies. There were newspapers and magazines around for the customer who might need reading material while eating alone. The normal table setup could include a constantly varying assortment of toys and puzzles—a custom that started when the Shopsins' children were young and continued for the more or less grown-up customers. The counter was taken up mainly by buckets of complimentary penny candy. One wall had, in addition to a three-dimensional advertisement for Oscar Mayer's beef franks, some paintings of the place and its denizens. The portrait of Kenny showed him as a bushy-haired man with a baby face that makes him look younger than his age and a girth that may reflect years of tasting his more remarkable creations; he's wearing a SHOPSIN'S GENERAL STORE T-shirt, folded over in the way the cognoscenti know to fold it in order to form the words EAT ME. A large sign behind the tiny kitchen that Kenny shared with his longtime assistant, José, said, ALL OUR COOKS WEAR CONDOMS. When I had taken in all of that, or whatever part of it was there at the time, I said, "I absolutely agree, Eve. A reviewer might comment on whether or not the decor is to his taste. Conceivably, he could prefer another type of decor. But you can't say that this place has no decor."

Mentions of Shopsin's in print have usually been complimentary, in a sort of left-handed way—as in *Time Out New York*'s 2002 guide to the city's restaurants, which raved about the soups and mentioned Kenny ("the foul-mouthed middle-aged chef and owner") as "a culinary genius, if, for no other reason than he figured out how to fit all his ingredients into such a tiny restaurant." To Kenny's way of thinking, a complimentary mention could be worse than a knock. It might attract review trotters—the sort of people who go to a restaurant because somebody told them to. These are more or less the same people Jim Leff has in mind when he talks about "Zagat-clutching foodies," and Kenny doesn't like them any more than Leff does. Kenny had found that review trotters are often "petulant and demanding." Failing to understand that they are not in a completely conventional restaurant, they may be taken aback at having the person next to them contribute a sentence or two to their conversation or at hearing Kenny make a general remark in language not customarily heard in company unless the company is in a locker room or at being faced with deciding among nine hundred items and then, if they have selected certain dishes, having to indicate degree of spiciness on a scale of one to ten. (Before Shopsin's began restricting its serving staff to Eve, it employed a waitress who narrowed at least that choice by refusing to take an order higher than a six, on humanitarian grounds.)

Ken and Eve have found that review trotters often don't know their own minds. If a customer at Shopsin's seems absolutely incapable of deciding what to order, Eve, in the interest of saving time, has usually been willing to reveal her own favorites. (For a while, those happened to be three dishes with chicken in them—Chicken Tortilla Avocado Soup, Pecan Chicken Wild Rice Cream Enchilada, and Taco Fried Chicken.) But she doesn't do it with a song in her heart. Kenny is less flexible. "If somebody comes in here and is flabbergasted by the number of things on the menu and tells me, 'How can I choose?'" he once told me, "I realize that they're essentially in the wrong restaurant."

The restaurant that Ken carved out of the old Bubble Gum Store, at Bedford and Morton, could handle just so many people, and he was never interested in an expansion that would transform him into a supervisor. "The economic rhythm of this place is that I run fifteen meals a week," he often said, before Shopsin's, after twenty years of operation, started offering Sunday brunch. "If I do any five of them big, I break even; if I do ten of them big, I'll make money. But if I do fifteen I have to close, because it's too much work." Kenny requires slow periods for recouping energy and ingredients. The techniques that enable him to offer as many dishes as he offers are based on the number of people he has to serve rather than on what they order. That's why he decided not to do takeout and not to serve groups larger than four. Pretending to be a party of three that happened to come in with a party of two has always been a very bad idea.

Not all the rules at Shopsin's came about because of limitations on how many meals the kitchen could put out. For years, for instance, a rule against copying your neighbor's order was observed fairly strictly. Customers who had just arrived might ask someone at the next table the name of the scrumptious-looking dish he was eating. Having learned that it was Burmese Hummus—one of my favorite dishes, as it happens, even though it is not hummus and would not cause pangs of nostalgia in the most homesick Burmese—they might order Burmese Hummus, only to have Eve shake her head wearily. No copying. That rule eventually got downgraded into what Ken called "a strong tradition" and later became unenforced except, I suppose, for special occasions. "I realized that the problem was not that they were trying to imitate the other person but that they weren't capable of ordering anything themselves, and it was just unnecessary cruelty to point that out to them," Kenny told me. He said he was getting more and more people of that sort.

"Why is that?" I asked.

"The country's going that way," he said glumly.

Shopsin's developed a number of rules, not all of them completely black and white. When New York City imposed smoking restrictions that exempted restaurants with fewer than thirty-five seats, for instance, Kenny posted a sign saying SMOKING OK and posted next to it a sign-up sheet headed something like "Unless One of the Following People Is Here." Because of the rules and because Kenny is, by his own admission, "not a patient person," I've occasionally run into people who were afraid to enter the place. I've escorted a number of them to their first Shopsin's meal, in the way a longtime businessman in a midwestern town might escort a newcomer to Kiwanis on Wednesday. Since the *Seinfeld* Soup Nazi episode became part of the culture, people sometimes compare Kenny with the brilliant but rule-obsessed soup purveyor Jerry Seinfeld tried to deal with. Kenny would say that one difference between him and the Soup Nazi is that the Soup Nazi is shown ladling out his soup from a steam table; at Shopsin's, the soup has always been essentially made from scratch when it's ordered.

Also, some people think of Shopsin's as forbiddingly clubby, chilly to outsiders. Actually, Shopsin's does not have a crowd, in the sense of a group of people who go in assuming they'll meet someone they know—the way the old Lion's

Head, a few blocks up Seventh Avenue, had a crowd, built around *Village Voice* writers. At a play reading once, I was surprised to run into a Shopsin's regular I hadn't realized was an actor; all I'd known about him was that he doted on a dish called Turkey Spinach Cashew Brown Rice Burrito. Still, there are a lot of regulars, and they seem more at home than they might at a conventional restaurant. "You're really not allowed to be anonymous here," Kenny has said. "You have to be willing to be who you really are. And that scares a lot of people." One evening, when the place was nearly full, I saw a party of four come in the door; a couple of them may have been wearing neckties, which wouldn't have been a plus in a restaurant whose waitress used to wear a T-shirt that said, DIE YUPPIE SCUM. Kenny took a quick glance from the kitchen and said, "No, we're closed." After a brief try at appealing the decision, the party left, and the waitress pulled the security gate partway down to discourage other latecomers.

"It's only eight o'clock," I said to Kenny.

"They were nothing but strangers," he said.

"I think those are usually called customers," I said. "They come here, you give them food, they give you money. It's known as the restaurant business."

Kenny shrugged. "Fuck 'em," he said.

Anytime there seemed to be a threat of becoming entangled in a piece of unauthorized publicity about Shopsin's myself, I have resorted to rank cowardice, spooked by the fear of a life-time banishment that might not even carry the possibility of parole. Once, I asked Kenny if an acquaintance of mine who'd been eighty-sixed some years before but greatly missed the place and its proprietors could come in for lunch with me sometime. "Sure, she can come in for lunch," Kenny said. "And I'll tell her she's a scumbag bitch." I told him I might hold off on that lunch for a while.

In the middle nineties, I got a phone call from a reporter named D. T. Max, who was doing a piece for *The New York Observer* on Shopsin's, without the cooperation of the proprietor. After assuring him of my belief that reporters have an obligation to talk to other reporters on the record and informing him that I had been quoted by name insulting most of the people I've ever worked for, I told him that in this instance I intended to be exceedingly circumspect and to keep Kenny informed on everything I said. Max was most understanding.

When I did report back to Kenny, I was asked what information I had surrendered. "Well, the subject of Egyptian Burritos came up," I said. Egyptian Burrito was then listed on the breakfast menu, although I'd never actually eaten one. On the rare occasions I had been to Shopsin's for what people in some other trades might call a breakfast meeting, I'd always allocated my calories to Shred Potatoes, a fabulous dish that Kenny claims to have stolen from a short-order cook in the Carolinas through intense observation that required only ten minutes. Still, I liked the idea of an Egyptian Burrito enough to lodge a complaint some months later when it was dropped ("It's getting to be like a Howard Johnson's around here; you can't even get an Egyptian Burrito for breakfast").

"And?" Kenny asked.

"Well, he seemed interested in what an Egyptian Burrito was," I said.

"So what did you say?"

"I said 'An Egyptian Burrito is a burrito and inside is sort of what Kenny thinks Egyptians might eat.'"

Kenny considered that for a moment. "Well, that's accurate," he finally said. He sounded relieved. By chance, though, the *Observer* piece ended with an anecdote, accurately gathered from someone else, that involved me: One morning, a Sanitation Department officer had come in to ticket Kenny for some minor infraction like wrapping his garbage incorrectly or putting it in the wrong place. Kenny, who was at the stove, lost his temper—he's always had what he calls "a little trouble with authority"—and threw a handful of flour he happened to be holding at the Sanitation officer, who thereupon summoned a police officer to write a citation. When I was told about the incident at lunch that day, I'd asked Kenny, "What was the citation for—assault with intent to bake?" A couple of months after Max's item appeared, Kenny said that he had finally concluded that I, frustrated at not having been able to work the assault-with-intent-to-bake line in anywhere, might have instigated the *Observer* article just to get it into print. I had a defense for that: Within days of my exchange with Kenny about flour throwing, I had, without mentioning any names, eased the anecdote into a newspaper column that was on a completely different subject.

Yes, I'd managed to write about Shopsin's from time to time, always observing the prohibition against mentioning its name or location. That is one reason I'd never been offended by Kenny's refusal to recognize a reporter's God-given right to turn absolutely everything into copy. In a piece about Greenwich Village for a book celebrating the centennial of New York

City's unification, for instance, I asked a restaurant proprietor "who tends not to be cordial to people wearing suits" what the difference was between the Village and uptown, and he said, "I don't know. I've never been uptown." Kenny never objected to any of the mentions. He has always thought of us as being in similar fields, and, as someone who has to be prepared every day to turn out any one of nine hundred dishes a customer might ask for, he has a deep understanding of waste not, want not.

In the middle seventies, in fact, I wrote an entire article for *The New Yorker* about a corner store in the West Village that was run with rare imagination and a warm feeling for community—a store with a rocking chair and bean-counting contests and free circulating paperback books. The store, I wrote, struck me as being about as close as Greenwich Village got at that time to the Village conjured up by reading, say, *My Sister Eileen*— even to the point of having a proprietor, described in the piece as a young man from a prosperous background, capable of making occasional allusions to Camus or Sartre as he sliced the roast beef. I simply referred to Shopsin's by the name my girls always used in those days—the Bubble Gum Store.

So what changed to permit me to refer to it by its actual name? In the spring of 2002, Kenny told me that it was no longer necessary to abide by the rule against mentioning the place in print. The building that Shopsin's occupied, an undistinguished five-story brick structure that consists of a ground-floor commercial space and eight apartments, had changed hands. Kenny, who was faced with having to renegotiate his lease, at first treated the situation philosophically. When I asked him what the new owner, Robert A. Cohen of R. A. Cohen and Associates, was like, he shrugged and said, "He's a real estate guy," in the tone that New Yorkers customarily use to mean that asking for further details would be naïve. Then Kenny and Cohen had a meeting at Cohen's office ("I went uptown!" Kenny told me, as a way of emphasizing a willingness to put himself out). According to Kenny, Cohen offered the Shopsins a one-year lease at more or less market rent. He also offered a three-year lease, contingent on one of their daughters vacating a rent-stabilized apartment she occupied in the building. A one-year lease is obviously not practical for a restaurant, and the attempt to include Kenny's daughter in the transaction did not please him. All in all, I would say that Robert A. Cohen was fortunate that the offers were made when Kenny wasn't holding a handful of flour.

Kenny decided that he would leave at the end of the agreement he had—a date only a couple of months away. He was aware, though, that the tone of his business had a lot to do with the physical space it had occupied for more than thirty years, including what I suppose you'd have to call the decor. In other words, the Shopsin's my daughters had known—Kenny's, Ken and Eve's, the Bubble Gum Store—could no longer be affected by publicity because it would no longer exist.

The god of New York real estate is an ironic god, and he works in ironic ways. What had propelled Ken and Eve into the restaurant business in the first place, twenty years before, was a bump in their rent. They figured that their choices were to extend the hours of the corner store—they had always closed on weekends—or transform the store into a restaurant. By that time Kenny was doing a good business in take-out sandwiches like chicken salad and egg salad. "Zito would bring me over bread and I would just have a line out the door every lunchtime," he has recalled. "Essentially, if anyone asked me what I did for a living, I said I sold mayonnaise— mayonnaise with chicken, mayonnaise with shrimp, mayonnaise with eggs, mayonnaise with potatoes. The key was that essentially you sold mayonnaise for eight dollars a pound and everything else you threw in for free." He had also been making what he calls "restaurant-style food to take out of a non-restaurant"—turkey dinner every Wednesday, for instance, and chicken pot pie. When Ken and Eve closed the store for the summer—because they had young children, Shopsin's was the rare Village business that often observed the *fermeture annuelle*—Ken, a reasonably adept handyman who had worked as a building superintendent before he went into the grocery business, spent a month or so turning Shopsin's General Store into a restaurant. When it opened, the menu listed a conventional number of more or less conventional dishes, although there was some hint of the future in items like Yiddishe Melt (Grilled American cheese on rye over grilled Jewish salami) and Linda's Frito Pie, a Texas specialty whose recipe has to begin "Take a bag of Fritos . . ."

Kenny had Frito Pie on the menu because one of his customers, who's from Texas, was comforted by the knowledge that less than a block from her house in Greenwich Village she could order a dish that most Texans identify with the snack bar at Friday-night high school football games. The menu grew because of what customers wanted or what Kenny was struck by in reading cookbooks or what new ingredient he happened across or what he figured out how to do as he taught himself to cook. The young son of a Shopsin's regular always ordered either macaroni and cheese or pancakes, and one day, when he couldn't decide between the two, Kenny said, "Why don't you have both?" Macaroni and Cheese Pancakes found a place on the menu, listed between Macadamia White Chocolate Pancakes and Marshmallow Pancakes. "I don't make many decisions," Kenny once told me. "I react." At one point, for instance, a lot of dishes were inspired by the tchotchkes he'd bought on eBay. Because of some tortilla bowls he snapped up for a bargain price, he began offering Mexican Mu-Shu Pork, which could also be ordered with chicken or turkey and had something in common with a former dish called Thai Turkey Torpedo. Some large Melmac bowls split in two by a curving divider led to what he called Yin/Yang Soups—a couple of dozen soups and a couple of dozen kinds of rice that could be ordered in any combination, like Sweet Potato Cream Curry Soup with Piña Colada Rice or Toasted Pumpkin Seed Soup with Ricotta Pignoli Rice.

There was almost no danger of a customer ordering Plantain Pulled Turkey Soup with Strawberry BBQ Rice only to find out that there isn't any more Plantain Pulled Turkey Soup and he might have to settle for, say, Mashed Potato Radish Soup. In our family's twenty years or so of eating at Shopsin's, putting our meals on the tab we established when Ken and Eve were selling milk and paper towels and cat food, nobody at our table has ever ordered anything the restaurant is out of. When I asked Eve once if that held true with other customers, she said that she thought she remembered running out of chicken cutlets one time.

"I think I have everything all the time," Kenny has said.

"That's part of the system." What has happened occasionally is that Kenny gets an idea for a dish and writes on the specials board—yes, the specials board—something like Indomalekian Sunrise Stew (Kenny and his oldest son, Charlie, invented the country of Indomalekia along with its culinary traditions). A couple of weeks later, someone finally orders Indomalekian Sunrise Stew and Kenny can't remember what he had in mind when he thought it up. Fortunately, the customer doesn't know either, so Kenny just invents it again on the spot.

As the menu at Shopsin's grew over the years, I half-expected to come in for lunch one day and find Kenny being peered at intently by a team of researchers from the CIA—the Culinary Institute of America, that is—or maybe even by a team of researchers from the other CIA. The researchers would have their work cut out for them. If you listen to Kenny talk about cooking for a while, you can see the outline of some general strategies. For instance, he freezes preportioned packages of some ingredients that take a long time to cook and then pops them in the microwave—"nuking 'em" for a couple of minutes—while he's doing the dish. He fiddles with his equipment, so that he drilled out the holes on one burner of his stove and rigged up a sort of grid on another. He runs a new idea or a new ingredient through a large part of his menu ("I love permutations"). On the other hand, Kenny has said, "There's no unifying philosophy. I do a lot of things special, and not only do I do a lot of things special but I commingle them."

To get an idea of Kenny's methods, I once asked him how he made one of Eve's favorites, Chicken Tortilla Avocado

Soup, which he describes as a simple soup. "When someone orders that I put a pan up with oil in it," he said. "Not olive oil; I use like a Wesson oil. And I leave it. I've drilled out the holes in the burner so . . . it's really fucking hot. . . . On the back burner, behind where that pan is, I have that grid. I just take a piece of chicken breast and throw it on. The grid is red-hot, flames shooting up, and the chicken sears with black marks immediately and starts to cook. If there were grits or barley or something I would nuke 'em. . . . At that point in the cook that's what would happen if this were Chicken Tortilla Avocado with barley in it. For this dish—this is a fast dish—I shred cabbage with my knife. Green cabbage. . . . I cut off a chunk, and I chop it really finely into long, thin shreds. I do the same with a piece of onion. Same with fresh cilantro. At this point, José has turned the chicken while my back is still to the pan. I throw the shit into the oil, and if you rhythm it properly, by the time you have the onions and everything cut, the oil is just below smoke. Smoke for that oil is about 385. After 385 you might as well throw it out. It won't fry anymore; it's dead. But I turn around just before smoke and I throw this shit in. And what happens is the cabbage hits it and almost deep fries—it browns—and now we get a really nice cabbage, Russian-type flavor. The onions soften immediately, and I now turn back and I take one of any number of ingredients, depending on what they've ordered, and in this particular instance for someone like you, I would add crushed up marinated jalapeño peppers to about a five, which is about a half a tablespoon. They're in a little cup in front of me. . . . In front of me, in, like, a desk in-out basket, I have two levels of vegetables that don't need to be refrigerated and I have plastic cups full of garlic or whatever. So now the soup is cooking. So then I reach under the refrigerator. On the refrigerator floor there's another thirty or forty ingredients, and I'll take for this particular soup hominy—canned yellow hominy—and throw in a handful of that. Then I go to the steam table and take from the vegetarian black bean soup—it has a slotted spoon in it—a half spoon of vegetarian cooked black beans. And then I switch to the right, because the spice rack is there, and I put in a little cumin. Then I take the whole thing and I pour chicken stock in it from the steam table. And at this point José has already taken the chicken off the flame. The chicken now is marked on the outside and the outside is white, but it's not cooked. It's pink in the center. He cuts it into strips, we throw it into the soup, a cover goes on the soup, it gets moved over to the left side of the stove on a lower light, and in about three minutes José takes a bowl, puts some tortilla chips that I've fried the day before in the bowl with some sliced avocado, and then pours the soup over it. And that's Chicken Tortilla Avocado Soup." That's one of about two hundred soups, some of them not characterized as simple.

As we drew closer to the time when Ken and Eve would have to move or sign a new lease with Robert A. Cohen, I couldn't help expressing some concern. Presumably, Kenny could arrange his ingredients around a customized stove in some other storefront. Presumably, it would be convenient to my house. Still, who knew what jokes the god of New York real estate had left in his bag of tricks? What if, in some astonishingly ironic twist, a cheap storefront of exquisite funkiness became available on the Upper East Side? What if Kenny— who, despite being described as middle-aged in *Time Out,* was approaching sixty—decided that he wasn't up to starting in a new place? In our family, my son-in-law Alex was particularly worried. He and Sarah had planned their move back East some months before, but they were still in California. Alex was haunted by the fear that Shopsin's would close just before they arrived and that he would therefore never eat another Turkey in the Straw sandwich. Turkey in the Straw is pulled turkey that is mixed with coleslaw and barbecue sauce; it's served on a bun that can't quite contain it. After many meals at Shopsin's, Alex had finally tried Turkey in the Straw, and had decided that it was the single best thing he had ever eaten. But that had been on his last visit. He had eaten only one Turkey in the Straw sandwich in his entire life. How cruel, he thought, that just as he discovered his favorite it might be snatched from him. I didn't know how to put Alex's mind at rest on this subject. It's not as if I could assure him that, even if Shopsin's did disappear or move far away, he might find Turkey in the Straw at some other restaurant. That would be like saying that he might find Bugaloo-Shrimp Tabbuleh or Thai Chicken Sausage–Nut Quesadillas at some other restaurant.

I took to dropping in every day or two to take a reading of Kenny's plans. From what I could gather, he seemed to be giving serious consideration to two potential locations. One was convenient, but it was quite a bit larger than the former corner store, and it seemed less vulnerable to being shaped by Kenny's personality. Another had the appropriate funkiness but also had what everyone, Kenny included, believed was "the world's worst location." That was tempting to Kenny, of course. He is someone whose contrariness is so ingrained that he can begin a description of one cooking experiment like this: "At the time I was interested in baba ghanouj, I was reading a James Beard article about eggplants and he said never put eggplants in a microwave. So I went and put an eggplant in a microwave." When Kenny mentioned that the second place was on such an awful block that my daughters and I would probably come only once, I assured him of their loyalty, assuming he continued to turn out dishes such as "tomato soup the way Sarah likes it." Abigail and Sarah confirmed that when I phoned them to bring them up to date on the latest Shopsin's development. They also expressed some concern about the possibility that writing about Shopsin's even after the ban was officially lifted carried the risk of causing overcrowding or inadvertently saying something that could lead to the banishment of the author—and, presumably, his progeny.

"Don't worry about it," I told Sarah, as I finished my first article that would mention Shopsin's by name. "Kenny says it's okay."

"Just be careful," she said.

I was not eighty-sixed. In the weeks after the article appeared, Kenny did occasionally tell me that I was to blame for an excess of business or some other calamity. On the other hand, he was pleased at having come up with the intelligence that someone had sent a copy of the article to Robert A. Cohen's mother. "That was great," he said. "That was like a smart bomb." In July 2002, Kenny, resisting the siren call of the world's worst location, took a lease on the larger space he'd been considering. It's only a block or so away from the Bedford and Morton storefront where he and Eve had begun with a corner store thirty-two years before. The new space, on the corner of Bedford and Carmine, had previously been occupied for some years by a more conventional restaurant, a Middle Eastern spot called The Magic Carpet. The evening I got back from Nova Scotia, in early September, I went right over. Abigail and Sarah were eager for a report.

My first glimpse of the outside was, I'll admit, sort of a shock. Kenny had installed a bright green wraparound awning that said SHOPSIN'S in large white letters—an open invitation to strangers. Inside, another shock awaited me: Kenny chatting amiably with the eighty-sixed customer he'd threatened to address as a scumbag bitch if I brought her in for a rapprochement lunch. Either a general amnesty had been called in honor of the move or Kenny had mellowed. The decor did have some reassuring reminders of the old Kenny's. Some of the booths and paintings and memorabilia from Morton Street had been reinstalled, including the ALL OUR COOKS WEAR CONDOMS sign and the buckets of free penny candy and even a couple of the old corner-store shelves—nailed high on the wall and crammed with cans of beans and black-eyed peas and hominy. I was further reassured when Eve handed me the menu I was accustomed to—although I'd never had any reason to believe that Kenny might drop a few hundred items, the way some people sometimes misplace knickknacks in a move. There was also a specials board, done on paper held in an outsized clipboard, and the specials seemed to be Kenny-style—Thai Macadamia Chow Fun Soup, for instance. Eve recommended a special called Karma Roll, and I ordered it, deciding that inquiring into what it might be was not in the spirit of the evening.

A Karma Roll turned out to be something that looked sort of like a crepe and had folded into it a remarkably fresh-tasting green mélange with a spiciness I'd rate at about a four point two. When I asked Kenny about its origins, I received evidence that his R & D methodology hadn't changed. He'd seen someone at an Indian restaurant dip a single thickness of paratha into beaten eggs, put it in a pan, and, after flipping it, fold into it something the restaurant called cilantro chutney. Kenny realized that the same could be done with a flour tortilla. He invented his own filling, based on a machine he'd bought on eBay—a single-bladed hand mixer of the sort that is thrust into what looks like a water glass. Into the glass, Kenny puts fresh baby spinach, fresh cilantro, some jalapeño peppers that have been marinated in vinegar, coconut, garlic, mint, cumin, and a small amount of vegetable stock. Then, holding the blade at a particular place in the glass, he mixes the ingredients until they get what he calls fluffy, folds the mixture into the tortilla, and sprinkles curry powder on top. The result is so good that I decided it might replace Burmese Hummus as the dish I customarily order as an appetizer *pour la table* when I come in with guests.

Kenny hadn't attempted to re-create the precise atmosphere of the old place; "everything ends," he said. Although the space is considerably larger than the Shopsins' former restaurant, he had put in only a half dozen or so more places to sit, having decided to limit the capacity so he could carry on his method of cooking. That made the new restaurant seem roomy rather than cramped—the Morton Street space was sometimes compared to a small, cluttered cave—and that, along with huge windows on both Carmine and Bedford, gave it an inviting look. Kenny did harbor some nostalgia for the cave. He told me, with some pleasure, that a longtime customer and friend once brought her mother, who was visiting from out of town, to eat at the old place, and her mother, once she'd had a look in the door, stopped at the threshold, unwilling to enter. The loyal customer tried pushing her dear old mom through the door, but the mother, despite her advanced years, held her ground, twisting and turning to counter each shove. Kenny said the mother was like one of those dolls that snaps back into position no matter what you do to it.

Despite the nostalgia, though, Kenny said that he liked the new, more open place better. "Being open—like with your article—has not brought us grief at all, has not brought us difficult customers, has not brought us anything bad," he said. "It has actually livened up the place a bit. It's too early to tell, but I'm beginning to think that the whole exercise was a good thing."

I said I was going to call Sarah to tell her that a reporter did not always do harm—maybe even that the apt comparison when characterizing a reporter was not always a jackal or a blood-sucking leech. "I'm going to tell her that being a reporter is something like being a, well, a . . ."

"An evangelist," Kenny said. "A missionary evangelist."

Definitely mellowed. I phoned Sarah as soon as I got home. "Kenny said he's happy at the new location and he should have moved ten years ago," I told her.

"I'm glad to hear that," she said.

"He said my article was a good thing for the place and that being a reporter is sort of like being an evangelist."

"An evangelist?" she said. "Well, that might be pushing it."

12.

A VERY SHORT HISTORY
OF THE FISH TACO

—
—

It's not as if San Diego has ever called itself the Fish Taco Capital of the World. True, I have thought of fish tacos as a San Diego dish since 1996, when I wolfed down any number of them while observing an otherwise uneventful Republican National Convention. Also, it's generally accepted that San Diego is where fish tacos were first sold in this country— although, from the beginning, they were clearly labeled as having originated someplace else. According to the story printed on the menus of a San Diego–based chain called Rubio's Baja Grill, a local boy named Ralph Rubio, prodded by his father to "get off his surfboard and make something of his life," opened a fish taco stand in January 1983, using a recipe he had acquired several years earlier while surfing in Baja California during spring vacation. Rubio built that first

stand into a business that twenty years later had annual rev-
enues of more than $100 million—an entrepreneurial saga
that must be treasured by every college boy whose parents
have ever told him what a wasteful mistake he's making by
concentrating more on college breaks than on college.

Rubio's Baja Grill still offers, in addition to its specialty,
simple Cal-Mex food, but fish tacos are not limited to San
Diego places where the alternative is, say, a carne asada taco or
a quesadilla. In San Diego, it's possible to order a fish taco in
one of those outdoorsy Southern California wooden-deck
restaurants that feature, in addition to a number of microbrews
on tap, dishes like Asian Barbecue Spring Rolls and Grilled
Salmon on Focaccia. You can get a fish taco in the sort of pan-
eled hotel dining room where you might be asked if you'd like
an after-dinner brandy. Any type of restaurant in San Diego
may feel obligated to list a fish taco on the menu, in the way a
steak frites restaurant in Marseilles might offer bouillabaisse,
just in case. Still, a survey of the San Diego restaurant scene
would probably not be entitled "Beyond Fish Tacos," the way
a 1998 guide to St. Louis restaurants was called *Beyond Toasted
Ravioli* or the way a picture-caption block of text I once
noticed in a *New York Times* article on eating in Philadelphia
was headed "Beyond Cheese Steaks."

In other words, the fish taco is a local specialty but not a
local specialty that is welded to the identity of the city. A fish
taco in the classic San Diego presentation (fried fish on a corn
tortilla, with shredded cabbage and a dressing that is customarily identifiable as being in at least the extended family of mayonnaise) does not demand to be called a San Diego fish taco in
the way chicken wings in the authentic Buffalo presentation

(cut in two, prepared with enough hot sauce to permit classification as mild or medium or hot, accompanied by celery and a bowl of blue cheese dressing that nobody has ever figured out what to do with) demand to be called Buffalo chicken wings. Restaurants in San Diego present all sorts of embellishments on the fish taco concept—they may serve the fish grilled instead of fried, for instance, or include gobs of guacamole and cheese—but a veteran taco scarfer can't designate which version he wants by mentioning some long-established terms that aren't on the menu, the way someone in Cincinnati can order, say, chili on spaghetti with cheese and onions added by saying, "Gimme a four-way."

In some American cities, a local specialty that has deep roots can give an outsider the impression that he might need a codebook to order lunch. In Memphis, for instance, a barbecue eater who feels like ribs chooses a restaurant according to whether he prefers his ribs "wet" or "dry"—whether what is added at the last minute is sauce or a sort of dry rub of spices. He can order a particular kind of barbecued pork sandwich by saying, "Gimme a white pulled"—although I don't know why anyone would, since "white" is what people in Memphis call the lighter and juicier interior meat, and ordering it breaks the law of nature that states, "The crunchy part of anything's the best." Memphis people say "brown" if they want a preponderance of the crunchy part. "Pulled" means pulled off the bone—as opposed to "chopped," which is pulled meat cut up into finer bits. There is no such thing as "sliced": if a piece of pork shoulder could stand up to slicing, people in Memphis would figure that it needed four or five more hours in the pit.

Yes, there are places where I've found the concentration

on local specialties somewhat, well, relentless. On a trip to Jerusalem, for instance, I was reminded of eating in Turkey: On the first night you say, "Hey, that was pretty good," and on the second night you say, "Okay, but wasn't that something like what we had last night?" and on the third night you say, "What's going on here?" But if I had only one meal to eat in St. Petersburg, Florida, for instance, eating anything but smoked mullet would strike me as unsound. Unless, that is, I'd gotten a tip about a Chinese restaurant. Otherwise, I'm someone who insists on crabs when in Baltimore. I'm afraid my response to, say, a Tucson booster who has suggested that we dine in the most sophisticated new Tuscan trattoria in town would be, "But if we're in Tucson, shouldn't we be eating chimichangas?"

I like to think that I'm not an extremist in preferring the local specialty. If, while driving to dinner with some gracious hosts in Saginaw, I learned that we were heading toward what is widely considered the most distinguished restaurant in central Michigan, I think I could refrain from saying, "Stop the car! I will simply not allow my one meal in Saginaw to be anything but a chopped-peanut-and-mayonnaise sandwich." Although I grew up just a short drive from Kansas City, Kansas, I remained a stranger to what was once considered its culinary specialty—pig-snout sandwiches. I do have my limits.

Still, I'm less likely to be interested in sampling evidence that a city has gone beyond a local specialty than in investigating what might have been passed over too quickly. While I was in Philadelphia once on a short business trip, for instance, Craig LaBan, the restaurant critic of *The Philadelphia Inquirer*, learned that I had never had a roast pork sandwich in the

Philadelphia style—a crusty hoagie roll stuffed with thinly sliced pork and sautéed greens and sharp provolone and juice and some secret ingredients among which LaBan had detected not only garlic and rosemary but also clove. He saw to it that this deprivation was corrected at a place called John's, in South Philly, and as we finished our meal it occurred to me that in the great tournament to decide the iconic dish of Philadelphia, the cheese steak must have been fortunate enough to draw a bye instead of having to go head-to-head with John's pork sandwich.

San Diego does have some purists—the equivalent of those Philadelphians who treat with disdain a cheese steak whose cheese is not actually Cheez Whiz from the jar. On a trip I made to San Diego, a local architect named Wallace Cunningham, who designs spectacular houses in wealthy suburbs like Rancho Santa Fe and Del Mar and La Jolla, was kind enough to take my daughter Sarah and her husband, Alex, and me to some fish taco purveyors that various authorities had recommended. I had become curious about whether what I'd eaten in 1996 was an indication that San Diego is truly the place that fish taco fanatics must get themselves to if they feel a binge coming on. As a guide, Wally seemed to have the right spirit. When he got on his car phone to check the address of a place called Mario's de la Mesa, I had noted with satisfaction that, once the directions were straightened out, he followed up with the sort of questions a serious connoisseur might ask: "Are the fish tacos incredible? Will they change our lives?"

On our way to Mario's de la Mesa, we stopped for a fish taco at a hip-looking place called The Tin Fish, across from the Convention Center, and were given fried fish wrapped in a tortilla made of flour rather than corn. "I'm shocked!" Wally said, pushing the flour-tortilla taco away. I figure that it takes a lot to shock a man in Wally's line of work; anybody who doesn't faint dead away at hearing what, say, the master bathroom is likely to run one of Wally's clients is obviously a worldly person. But he seemed truly taken aback. He sat there shaking his head sadly and mumbling something about the importance of corn in Mayan culture, while Alex, in whom I've detected a pleasing flexibility at table, and I polished off the offending tacos.

On the other hand, I have never heard people in San Diego argue far into the night about where the best fish tacos can be found—the way I used to hear, in my boyhood, Kansas City people argue far into the night about the relative merits of the ribs offered up by Bryant's and Gates and Rosedale. San Diegans in large numbers obviously like fish tacos, but not to the point of thinking that someone who prefers the version at some other purveyor is a person of deeply flawed character. I suspect that conversations among San Diego residents about fish tacos are not intense conversations, and I suspect that conversations with visitors are more likely to be about the splendid climate or the state of the biotech industry than about the fish taco triumphs of Rubio's Baja Grill or Baja Fresh or Wahoo's or the Brigantine. In other words, these San Diego people, if I might be allowed to say so just this once, have other fish to fry.

It wouldn't surprise me, in fact, if a booster of San Diego as a sunny paradise for Nobel Prize–winning scientists and retired millionaires would respond to a question about fish tacos by pointing out that the geographical name commonly used by California restaurants to signal a specialty in fish tacos is not San Diego but Baja or Ensenada. Whichever American city it was that first served Belgian waffles is not the Belgian waffle capital of the world; that would be Belgium. All of which is to say that if the best fish taco I've eaten on this side of the Mexican border turned out to be in Los Angeles rather than in San Diego, it would not be a disgrace. It would be mildly embarrassing maybe, but not a disgrace.

"This is not a disgrace," I said to Alex, as he and Sarah and Wally and I finished up our multistop lunch in San Diego with some fish tacos at the original stand opened by Ralph Rubio, in an area of San Diego called Mission Bay. Alex and I agreed, though, that nothing we'd eaten in San Diego could match some fish tacos we'd eaten the day before, during a sort of warm-up expedition in Los Angeles. After trying out a couple of chains in Marina del Mar, we'd headed for East Los Angeles to eat at Tacos Baja Ensenada, a place that had inspired Jonathan Gold to write in *Counter Intelligence*, "Entire religions have been founded on miracles less profound than the Ensenada fish taco." Tacos Baja Ensenada turned out to be a cheerful corner restaurant on Whittier, the broad boulevard that cuts across East L.A. We ordered a few fish tacos and took them to one of the outdoor tables. After our first few bites, I could see by Alex's expression that he'd converted to the fish taco faith conjured up by Gold. I was having quasi-religious flashes myself: when I glanced across Whittier and spotted a Taco Bell, I mused on the possibility that it had been placed there by the Devil himself as a last crack at diverting pilgrims who are about to reach the real article. We decided, as a way of celebrating our first sacrament, to order a shrimp and octopus cocktail and some shrimp tacos. Those, in turn, made us so happy that we went to a bakery across the street and bought a couple of tamales.

Which is not to say that the fish tacos at the original Rubio's—or at Mario's de la Mesa, for that matter—were, in fact, a disgrace. Rubio's, even as a chain operation, manages to produce a batter whose crunch must have been a large part of the success fish tacos had on this side of the border. The similarity of the batter to tempura has been mentioned by people who believe that Japanese fishermen in Baja California might have had a role in inventing fish tacos. In a taco stand called Vida Mexicana in the food court of Water Tower Place, in Chicago—the farthest from Southern California I'd ever consumed a fish taco, although it turns out that Baja Fresh has outlets as far east as Virginia—I once saw a sign recounting a legend of origin: "A long time ago, on Baja's coast, in a small fishing village called Ensenada, Tia Maguí and her husband started serving whole fried fish. One day a Japanese man wandered by and offered a unique batter. They never learned the man's name and never saw him again, but out of that recipe came the legendary fish taco." If the published recipes for fish tacos I've seen are any guide, the mysterious Japanese gentleman may have been hanging around with surfers on college break, since one of the essential ingredients of his batter was beer.

Whatever ingredients were in the first fish taco ever sold, there is widespread agreement that it was indeed sold in Ensenada. San Diego fish tacos are a take on Ensenada fish tacos—

Southern California food with a vaguely Mexican theme, in
the way that those San Diego subdivisions with totally Spanish street names and totally Anglo residents are Southern California neighborhoods with a vaguely Mexican theme. Given
the Southern California concern with healthy eating, for
instance, Rubio's Baja Grill announces that its fish is fried in
noncholesterol canola oil and describes the dressing as a
"tangy yoghurt sauce." Baja Fresh has large signs in its restaurants saying, "No Microwaves, No Can Openers, No Freezer,
and No Lard." It describes what it serves as "Mexican-style"
food. If I wanted to taste fish tacos in their original version,
I'd have to go to Ensenada.

Ensenada is not, in fact, a small fishing village. It's a Pacific
port city of nearly four hundred thousand people, an hour or
so south of San Diego by way of an excellent four-lane high-
way. Its fish market is on a harbor that provides mooring for
dozens of sport-fishing boats. As in so many Mexican cities,
there is a *malecón* on the edge of the harbor—a seawall suit-
able for early evening strolling. Near the fish market, strollers
pass children who are tossing bait fish to half a dozen astonishingly noisy seals that tread water just off the rocks four or
five yards below—seals whose size can make you reconsider
the assumption that you wouldn't get fat if all you ate was fish.
The market has three lines of purveyors, every one of whom
had his wares displayed as if he'd received a tip that the
colonel of the entire regiment was about to pull a surprise
inspection. Some of the fish were already in fillets, and next to
some of the fillets—always the *angelito* and sometimes the

cazón, both of which are species of small sharks—there were hand-printed signs that said, POR TACOS.

I found fifteen or twenty bright little seafood restaurants pushing up toward the market in the way that lawyers' offices in a county seat push up toward the courthouse. All of them, according to their menus, provide fish soup and the Ensenada version of ceviche (fish and tomatoes and onions and coriander, chopped fine and spread on a tostada) and cocktails made with any of the remarkable variety of shellfish available by the basketful a few yards away. But their true specialty was obvious at first glance. Lined up on each table, in a row almost as precise as the fish displays in the market, were the fixings for fish tacos—shredded cabbage, whole radishes, whole peppers, chopped tomatoes and onions, carrots, white sauce, lime wedges, five or six kinds of homemade salsa, puree of avocado, a bouquet of coriander. These people, I realized, were serious.

In Ensenada, I found an intense interest in fish tacos well beyond the fish market area. Just off Juarez, a downtown street where locals go to buy clothing and shoes and groceries, substantial wooden stands like Tacos El Fénix draw crowds all day long—businessmen, kids in their school uniforms, construction workers on a break. The stands even have a special device for frying the fish. It looks like an outsized aluminum pot lid that's been turned upside down, with a high lip and a slight slope toward a little pond of oil that's positioned over the flame. The pieces of just-fried fish are placed on the warm aluminum around the pond, like tourists sunning around a swimming pool—although in a place like Tacos El Fénix they don't stay there long.

The taco I had at El Fénix was, by my rough count, the

sixth or seventh I'd had for the day, and the sun was still high in the sky. I had to admit that when I took the first bite of every one of them my thoughts turned to a meal I'd once had in Japan, in one of those restaurants where the chef hands you the tempura, piece by piece, as he finishes his work with it. Those thoughts visited me even though I'd been told on good authority (the proprietor of a fish-market restaurant called Mariscos El Norteño) that the fish taco was invented not by anyone from Japan but by a fisherman from Guerrero province who was known to everybody as Huachivalato. I can't be certain who invented the fish taco. I am certain, though, that Ensenada is the Fish Taco Capital of the World.

When I returned to San Diego, I had time for one more dinner. I was planning to extend my fish taco repertoire in the company of Tom Chino and his wife and some friends of theirs. Tom is the proprietor of Chino Nojo Inc. in Del Mar, a farm whose vegetables and fruits are legendary in the food world. He is also known as a serious eater. When he picked me up, he asked if I was absolutely committed to having more fish tacos. I considered that question for a moment. There were still a couple of highly recommended fish taco places I wanted to try. The other possibility, Tom went on to say, was a Chinese restaurant.

A Chinese restaurant?

Tom said that the restaurant he had in mind was a Szechuan place called Spicy City—a favorite of his and of the Chinese scientists who work in the biotech industry and the University of California at San Diego and the Salk Institute. I

took in that information. I couldn't help thinking of Star
Twinkles. Aside from academic degrees and pay scale, after
all, what was the difference between the Chinese scientists in
San Diego and the Chinese contract workers who mined phosphate in Nauru? Going to a Chinese restaurant wouldn't be
the equivalent of leaving St. Petersburg without any smoked
mullet at all, I told myself. I'd eaten plenty of fish tacos. Also,
what was the likelihood of finding a fish taco superior to those
at Tacos Baja Ensenada, let alone the ones I'd had in Ensenada
itself? And what would that prove? I had already decided that
fish tacos were not central to the identity of San Diego. Ensenada is the Fish Taco Capital of the World.

Twenty minutes later, we were at one of those L-shaped
malls that have been carved into the corners of so many wide
Southern California intersections. The signs on many of the
stores were in Korean or Chinese as well as English; a sign
identified the mall itself as Plaza del Sol. There were five of us
at Spicy City, and we ordered Husband & Wife (beef and
tripe), Sesame Peanuts, Lau Hu Cai (cilantro and julienne of
bell pepper), Spicy Boiled Pork, Mongolian Beef, Shrimp in
Garlic Sauce, Chef's Special Green Beans, Ants Climbing
Trees (braised rice noodles with ground pork), and a Wonton
Soup so good that it should have been called something else.
Even with all that, we came pretty close to being what the
intellectuals call Clean Plate Rangers. As we sat back, stuffed
and satisfied, I realized what we had just done. We had gone
beyond fish tacos.

13.

BARBECUE AND HOME

——

When I haven't been back to the haunts of my boyhood for a while, Kansas City barbecue might be expected to leap to the top of my Register of Frustration and Deprivation. It doesn't. For me, Kansas City barbecue turns out to be in a category of its own: food that can be eaten only in its place of origin. People who travel thousands of miles to avail themselves of the healing waters found in a single miraculous spring have good reason for not trying to make do with a bottled version in a more convenient location. Over the years, when I've been asked if I can make any recommendations for someone who lives in New York and wants a taste of Kansas City–style barbecue, I always say, "Catch a cab to Queens, get off at La Guardia Airport, and fly to Kansas City." If someone opened a restaurant that managed to reproduce Kansas City barbecue around the corner from my house—somehow obtaining the right easements from New York City environmental laws and the right hardwood and the right barbecue pit and the right pit master, somehow shaking off the widespread assumption that eating barbecue in lower Manhattan is like eating *soupe au poisson* in Sioux Falls—I would not rush right over. I'd be grateful to have a Memphis barbecue joint or a North Carolina barbecue joint or a Texas barbecue joint around the corner. Not a Kansas City barbecue joint. I eat Kansas City barbecue in Kansas City, as often as possible. When I visit my sainted hometown, the old friends I customarily have dinner with long ago quit bothering to suggest that we go to someplace like Kansas City's most sophisticated new Tuscan trattoria— which I assume, sight unseen, has much in common with Tucson's most sophisticated new Tuscan trattoria. There is no gushing about a recently opened bistro that serves sublime tuna carpaccio. My friends take for granted my intense longing for Kansas City barbecue—so much so that they think of my occasional willingness to eat some of my hometown meals in a fried chicken joint as reflecting a broader worldview than they have always associated with me.

Because barbecue is connected so strongly to place, it has always inspired a certain amount of local chauvinism. Have I engaged in any of this smoky braggadocio myself? Are the beef brisket sandwiches and short ribs I eat in my hometown heavily laced with nostalgia? Was I accurately described by a newspaper reporter and trencherman I'll call Charlie Plum when he referred to me in print as someone who "has built a career on exaggerating the virtues of his hometown's barbe- cue"? Well, yes, of course. In the late seventies, for instance, John and Karen Hess mentioned in a *New York Times Magazine* article that they had visited Arthur Bryant's restaurant in Kansas City and had come away disappointed. In a letter to the magazine, I offered a simple explanation: Seeing a couple as distinguished-looking as the Hesses approach, the counterman in charge of pulling over a plate with one hand and throwing on ribs with the other hand had reached under the counter for some tongs, last used for a visit of the Emperor Haile Selassie in 1938. What nobody told the Hesses was that about forty percent of the taste was in the counterman's hand.

Despite what was implied by Plum, who grew up in Akron at a time when that city was noted for fashioning objects out of rubber in both its tire factories and its restaurants, a little local pride is nothing to be ashamed of. For years, whenever I returned to New York from visits to North Carolina and failed to bubble with enthusiasm while reporting on my barbecue eating to the displaced Carolinians I knew, they would question me about precisely where in the state I'd been. Then they'd solemnly inform me that I had eaten west of Rocky Mount and the superior barbecue in North Carolina is east of Rocky Mount—unless I'd been east of Rocky Mount, in which case I was informed that every bit of the North Carolina barbecue you wouldn't throw rocks at is found west of Rocky Mount. I finally concluded that someone who grew up in Kansas City is unlikely to make it to the right side of Rocky Mount.

Once, when I had business in Austin, I asked my eldest nephew, Cary Fox, who had recently moved to San Antonio after spending virtually all of his life in Kansas City, to meet me at Lockhart, world headquarters for the type of barbecue that originated in Texas meat markets run by German and

Czech butchers and is still served (on butcher paper) with no sauce at all. Cary is a strong Kansas City barbecue loyalist whose prenuptial dinner, if that's what that event was, took place at Bryant's; I know that because I had the honor of being the host. When Cary walked into Kreuz Market, where a sign says that the management deals in neither sauce nor forks nor side dishes nor credit cards, I noticed he had a small ice pack on his belt and I asked him what was in it. "A bottle of Bryant's and a bottle of Gates's," Cary said. Always a prudent lad, he was taking no chances. I pointed out another sign to Cary that said, "Do Not Bring Your Own Food onto These Premises." Cary was unimpressed. "It's not food," he said. "It's sauce."

Like Cary, I had always thought of myself as a hometown traditionalist when it comes to barbecue. The picture I carried in my mind of a barbecue man looked very much like Arthur Bryant—a calm, self-assured black man who was born in Texas in the early years of the twentieth century and died in his restaurant, in Kansas City, Missouri, eighty years later. By that time, the boosters among Kansas City businessmen—the people who hated my hometown's lingering image as a midwestern cowtown that had been known as "The Heart of America" and pushed the civic slogan "More Boulevards Than Paris, More Fountains Than Rome"—had begun to make their peace with the fact that the best-known restaurant in town was not some continental cuisine palace that had been treated respectfully by the AAA guide but a modest barbecue joint in a chancy neighborhood. A couple of days after Mr. Bryant's death, *The Kansas City Star* ran an editorial cartoon showing him being welcomed at the pearly gates by St. Peter, who has put his arm around Mr. Bryant's shoulder and is smiling in an ingratiating way. St. Peter is saying, "Did you bring sauce?"

Disagreement on the place of barbecue in the civic hierarchy was one reason my relations with the boosters were at times edgy. I didn't really make my peace until the late nineties, many years after I'd left home. At a banquet of the Chamber of Commerce, I finally explained how I might have been misunderstood a couple of decades before when I made a suggestion that apparently irritated some of the boosters—that one of the fountains they kept talking about could be dismantled and the material used to erect a monument to Henry Perry, Arthur Bryant's mentor, who brought barbecue to Kansas City. "It actually depended on how *many* more fountains than Rome we had," I told those assembled for the banquet. "If we had only one more, I didn't want to tear it down. I didn't want to lose the edge. I didn't want to arrive in Rome someday and find a sign saying, '*Più fontane di Kansas City.*'"

In my own way, I'm a booster myself. In fact, at that same banquet, I suggested another motto for my hometown, based on a study that had listed Kansas City as number four among the most obese cities in the United States: I said the Chamber of Commerce might consider erecting a sign at the airport saying, "Welcome to Kansas City: Fourth Fattest." I think it's the sort of greeting that could help put a traveler at his ease. The excess poundage in Kansas City, by the way, was widely attributed to the sort of food Kansas Citians prefer; the general manager of Gates Bar-B-Q was quoted in *The Kansas City Star* as saying that California cities finished low in the survey because people out there eat mainly "roots and bark." I think it was also attributable to the fact that Kansas City tends to finish last among American cities in surveys of how much the average restaurant dinner costs. As I envision the scene, one of my high school friends who's been presented the check for a huge fried chicken feed at say, Stroud's, says, "You know, we could order this meal all over again and still not spend as much as we'd spend in New York." There's a moment or two of silence. "Well, okay," someone in the party finally says, "but let's go a little heavier on the gizzards this time."

Mr. Bryant could surprise you. Once he told me that for some years he occasionally took advantage of being closed on Sundays by going straight to the airport after he locked up on Saturday night, catching a late flight to Dallas (this was before deregulation, of course, when late flights existed), connecting with a flight to Mexico City, and taking in a bullfight before heading back to Kansas City. By and large, though, I saw him as a single-minded man who stayed close to the premises, keeping an eye on the barbecue pit. I have been reluctant to permit much deviation from that model. In the mid-nineties, for instance, someone sent me an article from *Nation's Restaurant News* that was headlined "Equipment Advances Inspire New Breed of BBQ Operators," the equipment advances referred to being "convection ovens, combination steamers, and pressure smokers." The burden of the article was that this new equipment could replace the hickory pit of a traditional barbecue restaurant, resulting in great savings in labor costs, and could also make it possible to add some barbecue items to

the menus of restaurants referred to as "mainstream operators." A restaurant proprietor was quoted as saying of barbecue, "It's a good add-on, and I think we're going to see a lot of
pizza operators taking advantage of the opportunity."

At the time, I acknowledged a strong response to this
development in the restaurant industry—the sort of response
you might have expected from a lover of the old West who
had just read a headline that said, "Use of Electric Golf Carts
in Cattle Herding Inspires New Breed of Cowboy." One
thing I was certain I knew about barbecue was that it couldn't
be properly described as a "good add-on" or any other kind of
add-on; it's the main reason for being there. Another thing I
knew about it was that I wasn't looking forward to being
served any of it by some "mainstream operator" who also
serves pizza and burgers and clown napkins for the kids. A
third thing was that saying that labor costs can be held down
by not having it cooked slowly over a wood fire by a sullen
man with a squint was like saying that a symphony orchestra
would be cheaper without the violins.

I was aware, in fact, of a theory holding that long-term
proximity to a barbecue pit is an experience likely to melt
away the sort of bonhomie often found in a "mainstream
operator." Although Arthur Bryant occasionally gave a
Bryant's mechanical pencil to a favored customer—each pencil was dated by year and carried the motto "House of Good
Eats" and had a cow floating in clear liquid on the end; I've
been thinking that it's about time to put the ones I have in the
safety deposit box—a talent for marketing or packaging has
never fit my image of a barbecue man. Arthur Bryant once
said of Henry Perry, "He was the greatest barbecue man in the

world, but he was a mean outfit." When Fats Goldberg first tried L.C.'s, a barbecue joint that opened in Kansas City in the eighties, he ordered a beef sandwich and asked to have the sauce on the side. L.C. said that would be fifty cents extra. The fat man was mightily impressed. "A real barbecue guy!" he reported to me.

The prospect of barbecue being mainstreamed has not been the only development in recent decades that seemed designed to give barbecue traditionalists the willies. In the eighties, the good-natured boasting that has always been prevalent among true fans seemed to shade toward stilted remarks inserted by congressmen in the *Congressional Record* about the superiority of the barbecue found in their districts. Barbecue sauces with elegant labels began to appear in the gourmet classifieds and in the airport gift shops of legendary barbecue centers like Kansas City. Suddenly, there were so many barbecue-cooking contests that in certain seasons a competitive barbecuer could haul his rig from fairground to fairground like a man with a string of quarter horses. There was reason to be concerned that barbecue, like so much else in America, had become self-conscious and labeled and packaged and relentlessly organized and fitted out with promotional T-shirts.

Fairly early in the barbecue contest era—before there were sanctioning boards, before contests were held in such unlikely venues as New Holland, Pennsylvania, and Laughlin, Nevada—I attended a couple of contests, one in Memphis and one that is part of the festivities surrounding the American Royal Livestock Show in my hometown. Even then, some of the contestants had custom-built rigs the size of pickup trucks. A lot of them also had team costumes and antic team names. I suppose any negative remarks about barbecue contests could be considered unseemly coming from someone who, while visiting the Howlin' Hogs team of Millington, Tennessee, at the Memphis in May Barbecue Contest, ate as much of the whole-hog entry as I did. Still, I was always conscious of the fact that the iconic barbecue man I was carrying around in my mind—that is, Arthur Bryant, of Kansas City, Missouri— would probably not have been comfortable at such an event.

I don't say that because the customary demographics of a barbecue contest would make him one of the few black people in attendance. Even in the era when restaurants in Kansas City were segregated by a custom so entrenched that no signs were required, white people regularly showed up at Bryant's; in the later years of his stewardship, his restaurant attracted a clientele that was largely white. It was the tone of a barbecue contest that jarred with my picture of Arthur Bryant. Although a lot of the competitors have the deadly solemnity so often found in American hobbyists—so much so that a visitor is sometimes tempted to say, "Don't you think you're making too big a deal out of this?"—the contests also tend to attract the party-as-a-verb crowd. The atmosphere can be what you might expect to find at a keg party given by the fraternity most likely to be thrown off campus before the end of the semester. It wasn't easy to imagine Mr. Bryant in such an atmosphere, strolling past the huge rigs of barbecue teams with names like Peckerwood Point Paragon of Piggery or Ol' Hawg's Breath or Trichinosis Terry & His Borderline Swine or the Swine Lake Ballet or, in the case of a Graceland team at the Memphis contest, Love Me Tenderloin. On the other hand, it isn't easy to imagine Mr. Bryant in the stands of a bullfight arena in Mexico City, either. He could surprise you.

Despite my occasional rants, I never truly qualified as a barbecue purist. A barbecue purist, it turns out, is seriously interested in whether or not the proprietor of a barbecue joint chops his own wood. I was reminded of this, and of a lot more barbecue lore, at a gathering in Oxford, Mississippi, referred to by some of its participants as the Barbecue Summit—officially, the 2002 Southern Foodways Symposium. Charlie Plum was there. So was John Shelton Reed, a renowned sociologist of the South who compared barbecue with the cheeses and wines of France, in that a traveler through certain sections of the country can down an authentic version of the local variety for lunch and then encounter an entirely different variety by the time he reaches his dinner destination. So was Lolis Eric Elie, a New Orleans *Times-Picayune* columnist who wrote a book called *Smokestack Lightning: Adventures in the Heart of Barbecue Country*—a region that does not, in fact, include New Holland, Pennsylvania, or Laughlin, Nevada. There were talks about the role barbecue plays in politics and in race relations. Marcie Cohen Ferris, who grew up in Arkansas, discussed the barbecue deprivations facing southern Jews who observed the laws of kashruth; her speech was called "We Didn't Know from Fatback." Practitioners from several barbecue regions provided sustenance, and that turned out to produce a sort of epiphany for me: On the Saturday night of the summit, while tucking into the chopped pork provided by E. R. Mitchell of

Mitchell's Bar-B-Q, in Wilson, North Carolina, I realized that I had finally gotten myself on the right side of Rocky Mount.

It was my task at the summit to provide a sort of summary in the final talk, and the barbecue from Wilson, North Carolina, had put me in an expansive and ecumenical frame of mind. I said I deeply regretted that Marcie Ferris and the people she grew up with in Arkansas hadn't known about the Barbecue Easement granted by the Joplin Rebbe, a distinguished Talmudist and pit master. According to that wise teacher's ruling, observant Jews who are bona fide residents of the South and Lower Midwest are permitted to eat meat that has been subjected to slow direct heat for more than six hours and comes from any farm animal that does not have scales. I also revealed, before Plum and everyone, that on the question of barbecue traditionalism I'd come to the conclusion that I was a, well, moderate.

I hadn't been a moderate long. At least, it hadn't been long since I'd realized that I was a moderate. That realization had come in Kansas City. I was in town long enough for a couple of meals, and Doug Worgul, author of a book on the Kansas City version called *The Grand Barbecue*, suggested that we go to Oklahoma Joe's—a new place, which is to say it wasn't in operation when I was in high school. The lack of deep historical roots appeared to be only one of Oklahoma Joe's drawbacks. In the first place, it's just off Mission Road, one of the main thoroughfares of Johnson County, Kansas—a carefully maintained suburban county that the Kansas City writer Richard Rhodes, once he was safely out of town, labeled Cupcake Land. In places like Kansas City and Chicago, barbecue is essentially an inner-city specialty; I wouldn't ordinarily eat it

in Cupcake Land. Also, the proprietors of Oklahoma Joe's—
Jeff Stehney and his wife, Joy—are white. I am on record as
saying that in Kansas City going to a white barbecue joint is
like going to a gentile internist: everything might turn out all
right, but you're not playing the percentages. Also, Stehney
emerged from the barbecue contest circuit; his team, Slaugh-
terhouse Five, won eight grand championships in one year,
including the American Royal. Also, I'd read that he uses, in
addition to pecan wood, a device called an Old Hickory convection cooker. Also, what does Oklahoma have to do with
anything?

As we pulled up to Oklahoma Joe's, which is in a former
filling station that still sells motor oil and packaged beef jerky,
Worgul pointed out that it is actually on the southernmost
edge of Wyandotte County, abutting the Johnson County
line. Its mailing address is Kansas City, Kansas, although the
neighborhood didn't impress me as pig-snout sandwich territory. Worgul offered up no mitigating explanations for the
prize banners from barbecue contests displayed on the walls
and a menu that listed such foreign items as a Carolina-style
sandwich and a sandwich that had provolone melted on beef
with onion rings on top. Although the traditional barbecue
sandwich in Kansas City is beef brisket on cheap white bread,
Worgul was touting the pulled pork on a bun.

Partway through the pulled pork sandwich, I began considering the perils of rigidity. After all, Bryant's is now under
white ownership, and there's a branch at one of the casinos
planted in the Missouri River, and these days gas as well as
hickory is used. Did that mean I was going to avoid one of
Bryant's brisket sandwiches next time I was in town? Offering

a pulled pork sandwich was not the sort of thing Henry Perry would have done, but the world has shrunk; apparently, there is now a Memphis-style barbecue stand inside the University of North Carolina football stadium. You could say that this sort of thing is the barbecue version of globalization. And was I really opposed to technological progress, even if that progress included convection ovens? Stehney could hardly be accused of being what *Nation's Restaurant News* had called a mainstream operator; a man who entered twenty-three barbecue contests in one year is pretty tightly focused. When all was said and done, wasn't I in my hometown—or, at least, a few blocks from my hometown—eating barbecue?

"This is a pretty decent pulled pork sandwich," I said to Worgul. "I wouldn't throw rocks at this pulled pork sandwich."

14.

GRANDFATHER KNOWS BEST

⸻

Although a grandparent who arrives on the scene after the birth of a child is traditionally pictured cooking dinner for the sleep-deprived parents or stuffing the freezer with casseroles, I can tell you that these days it's mostly takeout. No, that is not simply the narrow view of a male grandparent who, admittedly, would have little to offer by way of home-cooked meals once he served the second dinner of meat loaf, accompanied by a salad of prewashed mesclun and a reminder of his mother's belief that meat loaf is one of the many dishes that always taste better the next day. As I was about to leave for San Francisco to inspect my daughter Abigail's first baby, my son-in-law's mother had just completed a similar visit, and Abigail reported to me, "We had some good sushi while Brian's mom was here." Brian's mother is not Japanese. Abigail was referring to take-out sushi—or "carryout," as they say in San Francisco, since, she warned me in advance, San Francisco is a place where restaurants are, in general, happy to prepare food to go but not happy to deliver it. In carryout, the accepted role for a visiting grandparent is to duck into the restaurant for the pickup while one parent waits behind the wheel of the double-parked car and the second parent remains at home, holding the baby with one hand and setting the table with the other.

The one exception, Abigail said, seems to be Chinese food, which does comes directly to the door. In Manhattan, the victuals customarily referred to as Take-out Chinese—essentially, a separate cuisine, if that's the word, from the food available in Chinatown—tend to make the trip from restaurants to apartment houses dangling in plastic bags from the handlebars of rickety bicycles. (The proprietors of Chinese restaurants apparently feel about baskets the way proprietors of National Hockey League teams used to feel about helmets—sissy stuff. The restaurant proprietors still feel that way about helmets.) Manhattan is essentially flat—I've been riding a bicycle around the city for at least thirty years, and I have yet to shift gears—but San Francisco is, famously, not. When my mind wandered during the flight from New York, I could picture one of those impassive delivery boys from a Manhattan Chinese restaurant trying to make it up a nearly perpendicular San Francisco hill, his determination unaffected by breathlessness or leg cramps or the fact that the weird angle has already caused a container of hot-and-sour soup to burst open on his trousers.

When my mind wasn't wandering, I was thinking about whether to present the home-delivery issue to Abigail as one more reason why it made sense to live in New York rather than San Francisco. I could imagine myself delivering the pitch: "Are you saying that you're willing to raise this child—this innocent child—in a city that has virtually no delivery, depriving her of the attention of whichever parent has to make the pickup or interrupting her schedule for a totally unnecessary car journey or, God forbid, cooking?" I could also imagine Abigail, who works as a legal-services lawyer for children, replying that, according to the laws and precedents she's familiar with, the sort of behavior I'd just described would not, strictly speaking, constitute child neglect.

San Francisco's lack of take-out delivery wouldn't have been completely out of place among the arguments I have used to bolster my case for living back East. After I'd arrived for my baby inspection, one of the first items that caught my eye on the bulletin board in Abigail's kitchen was a *New York Times* clipping I had sent her and Brian, who also practices law of the humanity-helping rather than the disgustingly lucrative sort, about young professionals who had left the Bay Area in the wake of the dot-com collapse. The subhead of the piece read "Dot-Commers Who Once Flocked to San Francisco Are Turning Elsewhere." I had pasted on an additional subhead of my own composition: "Many Lawyers, Complaining of Inferior Bagels, Are Also Leaving."

I suppose there are studies that connect the ubiquitousness of takeout in Manhattan with the increase in two-job families or the supposed hatred of cooking by yuppies, some of whom are said to live in expensive apartments that have no kitchens.

I have never actually run across an independently confirmed case of yuppies living in an expensive apartment with no kitchen, although a friend from that generation told me that he once sought to use the oven belonging to someone with whom he'd become romantically involved and found that she was using it to store fashion magazines.

It is also possible that the Manhattan restaurant industry simply came to realize that a city so compact that even prosperous families often do not own an automobile is an ideal place for developing a delivery business; literally thousands of customers live within a quick walk or a basketless bicycle ride from any restaurant. However it came about, it came gradually. When Abigail was born, in the late sixties, and her parents were thus sentenced for a while to a wearing but oddly pleasurable form of house arrest, the closest we got to takeout was for me to go to an accommodating Italian restaurant across the street and have them pack food in plastic containers that looked as if they were designed for some other purpose.

Sooner or later, though, the distribution of take-out menus became so relentless that a lot of New Yorkers began to see it as a form of commercially viable littering. I would guess, from my own experience, that most residential buildings in Manhattan receive menus from at least one restaurant every day. For a while, in fact, it was common in my neighborhood to see signs saying NO MENUS—sometimes in both English and Chinese. I never thought of posting such a sign myself. Yes, I occasionally get irritated when the steps in front of my house are littered with paper menus from two or three Chinese restaurants of the sort that seem to acquire their food from one gigantic kitchen, presided over in a dictatorial but not terribly inventive way by General Tso. But my attitude toward take-out menus is reflected in that brilliant slogan the New York State Lottery uses in its advertising: "Hey, you never know." It was a take-out menu, slipped through the mail slot of my door, that alerted me to a splendid little sushi restaurant on West Fourth Street called Aki, whose chef's experience working for the Japanese ambassador to Jamaica had inspired him to put on the menu a roll that includes both jerk chicken and hearts of palm.

Delivery by a restaurant of Aki's quality reflects a second stage of development in the New York take-out scene. When delivery of Chinese food consisted strictly of Take-out Chinese, for instance, I did not think of it as an acceptable alternative even to scratching around in the refrigerator for some leftovers that were way beyond what my mother would have considered their second-day peak. When we had some reason to eat our Chinese food at home rather than at a restaurant, I drove to Chinatown with my daughters and two or three of the dinner guests, everyone having been assigned to pick up a certain dish at a certain restaurant according to a split-second schedule—a food-gathering exercise we referred to as an Entebbe Raid.

Then, several years ago, Joe's Shanghai, a Queens restaurant that was noted for its soup dumplings, opened a Manhattan Chinatown branch that became a huge hit with the pasty-faced citizens the Chinese in America sometimes refer to, when in a benign mood, as "foreign devils." Soup dumplings, which on menus are often called steamed buns, get their name from the fact that the dumpling skin encloses not only a core that is often made of pork and crab—Jewish connoisseurs sometimes refer to soup dumplings as "double-trayf specials"—but also a liquid so tasty that diners tend to be sanguine about the clothing stains they acquire while trying to get to it. Not long after Joe's Shanghai appeared on Pell Street, Goody's, a rival soup-dumpling destination in Queens, established a Manhattan beachhead a few blocks away. Soon, a similar Queens restaurant called Shanghai Tang opened close enough to the Village to put my house comfortably within the delivery area.

Shanghai Tang—which, in the Chinese-restaurant name-changing custom that turned, say, New York Noodletown into Great N.Y. Noodletown and Chao Chow into New Chao Chow, soon became Shanghai Tide and then Shanghai Tide in Soho—listed on its menu, in addition to soup dumplings, dishes like Dry Fish Tripe with Pork Sinew. (Until some tweaking was done in the translation department a few years after the restaurant opened, that dish was actually on the menu as Dry Fish Stomach with Pork Sinus.) I don't often find myself yearning for Dry Fish Tripe with Pork Sinew, but I'm comforted by the notion that I live in a city where someone will bring Dry Fish Tripe with Pork Sinew to my door.

I wouldn't claim that Abigail was living in a neighborhood completely without eating possibilities. Several years ago, for instance, Yuet Lee, a restaurant on the edge of San Francisco's Chinatown, put a branch about three blocks from Abigail's house. Yuet Lee is a Hong Kong–style restaurant that turns out a spectacular version of fried squid—a dish I otherwise think of as routine bar food, often consumed by the sort of people who use their ovens to store fashion magazines. On a late afternoon in 1987, I was walking from an appointment near San Francisco's financial district when I discovered, by coming across little clots of people gathered in the streets, that the stock market had just had its largest single-day drop in history—what became known as Black Monday. Yuet Lee happened to be only two or three blocks away, and I went straight there. Within a few minutes, I was downing an order of fried squid that I had just watched emerge from the wok. It occurred to me that I might be the only thoroughly content person within several square miles. A branch near Abigail's house obviously enhanced my visits to San Francisco, but within a couple of years the branch closed. I managed to restrain myself from saying to Abigail, "I can't imagine what would keep you here now."

Why did I restrain myself? Because I'd like to think I'm above that sort of parental nagging. Also, I couldn't deny that Abigail's house remained within walking distance of the Mission—a neighborhood that is world headquarters for the San Francisco burrito. In San Francisco, the burrito has been refined and embellished in much the same way that pizza has been refined and embellished in Chicago. The San Francisco burrito, which is customarily wrapped in aluminum foil even if you have no intention of leaving the premises, is distinguished partly by the amount of rice and other side dishes included in the package and partly by sheer size. (*Out to Eat,* the Lonely Planet guidebook to San Francisco restaurants, describes a Mission burrito as "a perfect rolled-up meal," and

I would differ only in describing a Mission burrito as "two or three perfect rolled-up meals.") It is also so good that at times I've been tempted to put it on my Register of Frustration and Deprivation.

Serious eaters in San Francisco tend to be loyal to their own burrito purveyor. Abigail, for instance, is a Taquería La Cumbre person. In the spirit in which a rabid baseball fan from St. Louis might hand out Cardinals caps, she once presented me with a T-shirt whose front is almost totally taken up by La Cumbre's logo—a heroic painting of a sort of Latinized Ava Gardner wearing crossed bandoliers and carrying both a bugle and an unfurled Mexican flag. My childhood friend Growler Ed Williams, who teaches Spanish literature at San Francisco State, is a Taquería Pancho Villa person. I know perfectly respectable people whose loyalty is to Taquería Cancún, which is only a few blocks from Abigail's house. I have had terrific burritos at all three. I can understand a reluctance to leave a place within easy shooting distance of the Mission.

After a couple of days in San Francisco, in fact, I had to admit to Abigail that the Mission was a pleasant place for a grandfatherly stroll even aside from the availability of burritos: people raised in the Mexican culture know how to express their appreciation of a particularly stunning baby. As it turned out, a lot of the restaurants Abigail had selected for carryout were in the Mission. Some of them were outposts of gentrification, described by Abigail as "in the Mission but not of the Mission." So we might be picking up tamales one night, followed the next night by "seared dayboat scallops with organic spinach and black bean sauce." I wouldn't want to leave the impression that I thought eating carryout in San Francisco was a hardship. In fact, I tried to arrive at a fair appraisal to give Abigail as I left to catch my plane to New York. I finally came up with "It was okay for out of town."

Here's what I did when I got back to New York: I sorted my take-out menus. When I got through, I thought it was a pretty impressive collection. I had a wad of Indian and a wad of Mexican and a wad of Chinese (not just Take-out Chinese, either) and a wad of Japanese and a wad of pan-Asian and a wad of Italian and a wad of Middle Eastern and a lot of menus I found unsortable. I had about seventy-five menus.

I could picture Abigail on her next visit, glancing over as I placed the various types of menus in neat piles on the dining room table, like the organizer of a bank heist divvying up the loot. The Chinese pile, I notice, is about an inch thick. "What's your pleasure?" I say to Abigail. "Chinese? Thai? Indian? Middle Eastern? Venezuelan? Malaysian? Italian? How about some octopus salad and artichoke ravioli from Da Andrea? How about risotto? There's now a place on Bleecker Street called Risotteria that offers about forty kinds of risotto, delivered to your door."

Abigail shrugs. "I guess Italian would be okay," she says, still noncommittal.

"Or we could do what we call a walk-away," I say. "Limiting ourselves to restaurants within a few hundred yards of the house. It's a nice evening—we almost never get fog here—so maybe we could just stroll over and pick up, say, french fries at Petite Abeille or some zatter bread and marinated-chicken pitza at Moustache and bring them back here. If we feel up to walking an extra couple of hundred yards, of course, we could bring back lobster rolls from Pearl."

Abigail is beginning to pay closer attention. Maybe she had forgotten about Pearl's lobster rolls.

Then I'm offering all sorts of delivery possibilities— English fish-and-chips, Indian chaats, Japanese ramen, Singaporean fried rice. Menus are being flashed in front of her. I mention roasted chicken, the simple tuna fish sandwich, soup dumplings. Yes, soup dumplings! I tell her that if she'd like to finish off by having Cones, just around the corner on Bleecker Street, bring over a pint of hazelnut gelato, that, too, can be arranged. "I think it's fair to say, Abigail," I tell her, as I continue to flip through the menus, "that there's practically no type of food that can't be found within a few blocks."

Abigail shoots a meaningful look at my chest. By chance, I'm wearing the La Cumbre shirt she gave me. At least she thinks it's by chance. Suddenly, like Ricky Jay producing a ten of clubs out of thin air, I open a menu that has appeared in my hand. "Speaking of which, here's a place that might interest you," I say. "It's called Kitchen/Market, in Chelsea. You'll notice it says 'Delivery.'" I show Abigail the menu. Near the center is a group of ten items. The heading above them reads "San Francisco Burritos." Abigail looks very impressed.

ABOUT THE AUTHOR

CALVIN TRILLIN, a longtime staff writer for

The New Yorker, has written three previous books

on eating—*American Fried; Alice, Let's Eat;* and

Third Helpings. In 1994, those books were combined

in one volume, entitled *The Tummy Trilogy*.

He lives in New York.